FRENCH SECURITY POLICY IN A DISARMING WORLD

FRENCH SECURITY POLICY IN A DISARMING WORLD

Domestic Challenges and International Constraints

edited by

Philippe G. Le Prestre

with contributions by
André Brigot
A.W. DePorte
Edward A. Kolodziej
Philippe G. Le Prestre
John G. Mason

Lynne Rienner Publishers   •   Boulder & London

Published in the United States of America in 1989 by
Lynne Rienner Publishers, Inc.
1800 30th Street, Boulder, Colorado 80301

and in the United Kingdom by
Lynne Rienner Publishers, Inc.
3 Henrietta Street, Covent Garden, London WC2E 8LU

Library of Congress Cataloging-in-Publication Data

French security policy in a disarming world / edited by Philippe Le
Prestre; with contributions by André Brigot ... [et al.].

   Bibliography: p.
   Includes index.
   ISBN 1-55587-132-1 (alk. paper)
   1. France—National security   2. Nuclear weapons—France.
3. Nuclear arms control—Europe..   4. Nuclear arms control—France.
I. Le Prestre, Philippe G.   II. Brigot, André.
UA700.F78 1988   88-21703
355'.0335'44—dc19   CIP

British Cataloguing in Publication Data
A Cataloguing in Publication record for this book
is available from the British Library.

Printed and bound in the United States of America

The paper used in this publication meets the requirements of
the American National Standard for Permanence of Paper for
Printed Library Materials Z39.48-1984.

Contents

About the Authors

André Brigot is adjunct director of research at the Fondation pour les études de Défense nationale (Paris) and professor of economic and social sciences at the University of Paris. He is coauthor (with Dominique David) of *Le désir d'Europe: l'introuvable défense commune* and (with Renata Fritsch-Bournazel and Jim Cloos) *Les Allemands au coeur de l'Europe.*

A. W. DePorte is a visiting scholar at the Institute for French Studies, New York University. He served in the United States Department of State for twenty-five years. His most recent book is *Europe Between the Superpowers—The Enduring Balance.*

Edward A. Kolodziej is research professor of political science and director of the European Arms Control and Security Project at the University of Illinois Urbana/Champaign. A frequent contributor to professional journals, he is author of *The Uncommon Defense and Congress, 1945–1963; French International Policy Under De Gaulle and Pompidou: The Politics of Grandeur,* and *Making and Marketing Arms: The French Experience and Its Implication for the International System.*

Philippe G. Le Prestre is professor of political science at the University of Québec at Montréal. He is author of *The World Bank and the Environmental Challenge* and of numerous articles on international organizations, environmental politics, and foreign policy.

John G. Mason is completing his Ph.D. dissertation on "The Socialists and the 'Force de Frappe'" and teaches in the Department of Sociology of Queen's College (City University of New York). He coedited (with Guy Groux and Pierre Dommergues) *Les syndicats français et américains face aux mutations technologiques* and has written on French nuclear politics for *Telos* and other journals.

CHAPTER 1

French Security Policy in Its Domestic and International Settings

A. W. DePORTE

General de Gaulle's linked decisions, after his return to power in 1958, to build a French nuclear force under exclusively national control and to remove France from integration in the military system of the North Atlantic alliance were the objects of intense controversy in the 1960s, both within France and between France and other members of the alliance, above all the United States. By the 1980s, however, these policies had become the object of a nearly unanimous consensus among the French—including the Socialist and even (for a time) the Communist parties, as well as those of the right—and of acceptance, tinged with a certain degree of disinterest, by the Allies.

Now, in the late 1980s, there are circumstances suggesting that French security policy could again become a subject of contention at home and increased attention within the alliance. To understand the reasons for this, and to be able to explore the possible policy changes that may—or may not—emerge from such a debate, we need to consider both why the consensus came into being and why the policies it supported may no longer seem adequate, at least to some people, to meet France's security interests in the coming years. We are led, therefore, to consider how domestic and international factors combined to make French policy what it has been and, now, to challenge it. On the domestic side is the interplay of individual, party, and institutional factors and of public attitudes. Externally there is the evolution of the international system of which France is an important but interdependent member.

It is remarkable that this renewal of discussion about French capabilities and commitments with respect to security has emerged at a time when, unlike the case twenty-five or thirty years ago, French policy creativity, or assertiveness, on the international scene—as defined by the form and substance of de Gaulle's policymaking—has been diminished, or at least muted. While it has been a commonplace in recent years to describe as "Gaullist" the consensus among the major parties with respect to the foreign and particularly the defense policies that France has followed in this decade, in fact that description is only partly true. The consensus does include continued commitment to several of de Gaulle's highest priority policies, including a defense system based on the maintenance and expansion of a nuclear deterrent capability under French national control and France's assertion of its role as an independent player in European, alliance, African, Middle Eastern, and, indeed, world affairs.

But there have also been marked departures from de Gaulle's theory and practice (to be precise, from those particularly of the "high" phase of his policymaking, between the Cuban missile crisis in October 1962 and the Warsaw Pact's invasion of Czechoslovakia in August 1968). One of the most important is that in the 1980s coolness between France and the Soviet Union, rooted in both internal French and international circumstances, has replaced the former (real or alleged) "special relationship" between the two countries by which France, an ally of the United States but ostentatiously not a member of a U.S.-led bloc, asserted its importance as an independent player between the superpowers. For the same reasons there has been a realignment of France with the United States and its other allies with respect to, among other things, the deployment of intermediate-range nuclear forces (INF) in Western Europe and support for the Reagan administration's military buildup.

Official rhetoric has also been different from that which so characterized de Gaulle's foreign policy. Neither in the period of increased U.S.-Soviet tension in the early 1980s nor in the relaxation of tension that followed have French leaders seized the evident leadership opportunities offered them to insist that France, and Western Europe, define and defend their own particular interests in face of the challenges to them from both the quarrels and the cooperation of the superpowers. In European affairs at least, France consistently worked with the United States and the alliance and castigated Soviet policy. President François Mitterrand once said that anything that might help overcome Yalta (the traditional French phrase for the postwar superpower dominance of Europe) would be good, but that people should not mistake the wish for reality. That statement sums up very well the realism and, we might say, the adaptation to or acquiescence in the European structural status quo, so much decried by de Gaulle, which has characterized French foreign policy in this decade.

This attention to the tone of French policymakers in the 1980s is important, not only for what it can tell us about the substance of their policies, but because it draws our attention to the stark contrast with de Gaulle's use of style and rhetoric, along with policy itself, as intruments for raising the consciousness of the French people. De Gaulle tried hard, by word and deed, to convince the French (and others) that their country was truly in the first rank among the nations. For all his efforts, however, and all the changes that have taken place in the international system since 1945, or 1958, this has not been true since June 1940 and is not true in the 1980s. Mitterrand can refer to "the two powers that dominate the world" as to a fact of life and, whatever position one may hold in the ongoing debate about "continuity and change" in France, there are few French politicians who act or speak as if the nation had ceased to be itself because it is not, and no longer pretends to be, in the first rank. They think there is no point in denying that the Atlantic alliance and the European Community, for example, are important to France, or that the bonds of international interdependence—cultural and economic as well as political and military—have visibly become ever tighter in the 1980s. Such denials, so strong in de Gaulle's time as an impetus to a certain style of foreign policymaking, have practically vanished. It is enough for the French that they are able to believe that France is, as André Brigot puts it, at least "sovereign," if not fully independent, and is in a position—unlike most of its West European neighbors—to make the fundamental decisions affecting its own national life.

The institutions that de Gaulle led the French to adopt—those of the Fifth Republic—and other changes in the political system caused or catalyzed by his rule have contributed to this development. A broad consensus on foreign policy, partly on Gaullist lines, partly not, has been possible in the setting of a constitutional and institutional consensus, and such issues have been largely removed as a major source of division in the French body politic, which they were in de Gaulle's time (even as he tried to use foreign policy to neutralize domestic fissures) and before. Foreign policy issues did not feature significantly as such in the 1986 elections or in the 1988 presidential election.

This relative French "contentment" with the nation's place in the world is not, of course, necessarily permanent. But when we examine whether and how changes in French foreign or defense policy might come about, it is worth bearing in mind this record of recent years. Policy overall has been prudent, practical, and, on the whole, successful. In short, the French leaders of the 1980s have gone about protecting French interests in difficult times with a sense of limits and have done it well. French claims to great power status, once so ardently asserted and promoted by de Gaulle for reasons rooted in domestic as well as international considerations, have been muted. Rhetorical invocations of France's greatness have been few. What is more, this has been little contested among the political parties. Part of the foreign policy consensus of the 1980s, if seldom stated in so many words, has been to avoid these hallmarks of Gaullism as practiced by de Gaulle.

Why has French foreign policy, in form and substance, taken the turns it has since the 1960s? What factors may lead it in other directions, or keep it fundamentally on its present course? In a country so marked in recent memory by the impact of one great leader on its institutions and its policies, we are tempted to look first for the explanation of major changes, past or future, in the personal proclivities of other leaders. But French institutions have also changed, if not so much under de Gaulle's first two successors, Georges Pompidou and Valéry Giscard d'Estaing, then certainly since the transfer of power to the Socialists in 1981 and, even more, after the advent of cohabitation in 1986 (see chapters 2 and 3). And, of course, the international scene has also changed, from a phase of East-West détente in the early 1970s, to a revival of acute tension in the latter part of the decade and the start of the next, and then to what may be a kind of neo-détente in the last few years, symbolized—so far—by four U.S.-Soviet summit meetings and highlighted by the signing on December 8, 1987 by President Reagan and General Secretary Gorbachev of a treaty abolishing intermediate-range nuclear forces in Europe.

On one level, the discussion of the possible redefinition of the functions of France's military forces and the policies they are designed to defend has been motivated less by any of these developments than by the developmental logic inherent in France's fundamental policy, practically unchallenged, of possessing a plausibly credible deterrent force, together with conventional forces sufficient to protect French interests both inside and outside Europe. Attention to the role and possible uses of the nuclear force was almost certain to grow as its technical capabilities expanded. The details of its ongoing expansion are discussed in Edward Kolodziej's chapter. It is sufficient to note here that France will soon be capable of delivering many hundreds of nuclear warheads against targets in the Soviet Union (which is now recognized, unlike the case in de Gaulle's time, as the one threat against which the deterrent is aimed).

The credibility of the nuclear deterrent has been questioned over the years, but nuclear armament on this scale has to be taken seriously by both Soviet and alliance military planners, and somehow taken account of in U.S.-Soviet negotiations on the reduction of central systems.

At the same time, this growing French capability could not fail to be drawn also into consideration of the security position of Europe, and of the Western alliance, in light first of the deployment and then of the removal of intermediate-range nuclear forces. The French government did not choose to assert "independent" leadership in either of these developments—independent, that is, of the United States. It strongly favored deployment of U.S. missiles beginning in 1983, notwithstanding the theoretical temptation, which one might have thought would be particularly appealing to a Socialist government, to lead the many forces in Western Europe (and particularly in the Federal Republic of Germany) that were hostile to what they saw as a dangerous manifestation of superpower overlordship of a divided Europe. Nor has France resisted the U.S.-Soviet INF treaty, notwithstanding the dismay of some in Western Europe, and particularly in the Federal Republic, in face of this alleged "decoupling" of the United States, again in collaboration with the other superpower. But whether or not France continues to subordinate pursuing a European leadership role to working with the United States on major East-West issues, including arms control and alliance strategy, growing French capabilities will surely blend with the changes brought about by these and other developments to have an impact on evolving security and foreign policies.

We may conclude, then, that the late 1980s and the years beyond will be a time of reexamination for French security policy to an extent perhaps unparalleled since de Gaulle's innovations more than a quarter century ago. Will it also be a "period of transition"? If so, to what? For what reasons? And with what consequences for the domestic consensus on which policy has been based for the last decade?

In the chapter that follows, Philippe Le Prestre applies to French policymaking a set of hypotheses formulated by Barbara and Stephen Salmore which emphasize the importance of domestic political factors as sources of foreign policy. Clearly there is validity to such an approach, as is illustrated by the policymaking even of de Gaulle. Though he is often thought of as having the strongest personal preoccupation with France's international position and the freest hand in dealing with it of any modern French leader, he was surely also much concerned about the impact of what he did in this area—and how he did it—on the divided and demoralized French people whose leadership he assumed in 1958.

But to what extent can the evolution of French policy over the life of the Fifth Republic be explained by domestic variables? No one can doubt that de Gaulle's return to office had a profound effect on French foreign policy. Can the same be said for the changes of leadership in 1981 and 1986? If so, can the reasons for the policy changes be traced mainly to the personal choices of particular new leaders or to domestic political realignments?

In the case of the cohabitationist system of 1986-1988, when neither the president nor the prime minister had a free hand to conduct foreign policy, the hypotheses in question, as applied by Le Prestre, predicted that policy would reflect domestic political considerations to a greater extent than in the prior periods of presidential domination (characterized by the president's control of the National Assembly majority) and would be less coherent and less effective because of partisan political contention, bureaucratic conflicts, and inertia or stalemate among the policy-making leaders and entities. The results of such constraints would be "a reduced foreign policy activity and . . . lower levels of commitment."

Le Prestre demonstrates, however, that on the whole these predictions have not been validated by the record of French foreign policymaking after March 1986. That is not too surprising an outcome. For one thing, the hypotheses seem to overlook the important variable of the degree of consensus, or its absence, that happens to exist at a given time among contending forces with respect to foreign policy. There has been very considerable consensus in France on the main lines of foreign policy during the 1980s, so, even without taking into consideration the so-called "reserved domain" of presidential authority in this field, it is scarcely remarkable that there have been few important shifts since the March 1986 election.

Further, much of the policy on which there has been a consensus since 1981, as well as since the parliamentary elections, was already "lower," in Le Prestre's term, than the kind of Gaullist "higher" profile policies that are taken as the benchmarks for such comparisons. The very fact that there has been such a consensus since the early 1980s reflects, in turn, the hard fact, widely recognized, that France's options under whatever form of rule are considerably hemmed in by the international system in which it finds itself in the decade of the 1980s. This situation contrasts with that of the 1960s, when hopes such as de Gaulle's for systemic change to France's benefit, though eventually largely frustrated, could be propounded and even believed in with better reason.

Perhaps hypotheses linking foreign policymaking to domestic political configurations, while they are likely to have some degree of validity in any democratic regime, and in others too, may have greater explanatory and predictive power with respect to, for example, the United States (whose international options are more diverse than domestically imposed limits often make them appear to be) than to a middle power such as France, notwithstanding the example set by de Gaulle in relatively favorable circumstances. Certainly, foreign affairs have been less important issues in recent French presidential elections than they have been in U.S. elections, which may reflect a greater degree of consensus in the one case than in the other but also, and linked to that, a greater sense of limits or scarcity of realistic policy options in the French case.

This does not mean, of course, that a new French government will not make new policy or adapt old as international circumstances change. Mitterrand did so on a large scale after 1981 and made important changes that were so appropriate to the international setting and so acceptable to a broad consensus of the French people that the Chirac government found little opportunity or incentive to make further changes (with the principal exception of its efforts to "normalize" relations with Iran, which, however, also had a strong domestic political component related to terrorism and hostages). Whether or not U.S.-Soviet neo-détente persists, the second Mitterrand presidency can be expected to rethink the premises of policy that prevailed during the previous period of U.S.-Soviet tension and devise new policies and adapt old ones to the extent that circumstances so permit or require.

But Le Prestre's discussion of the repercussions in France of the Reykjavik summit and the continuing exploration of closer French-West German cooperation with respect to security shows the primacy of international developments for French policymaking over the change of government in 1986. If the differences on these matters up to now between the Socialist and the conservative parties have been quite small and adjustable, and if French initiatives in this area have not been as bold as some people might have liked, the reason seems to lie more in the inherent difficulties of, for example, taking long steps toward European defense cooperation—which has been on the agenda for more than thirty years—than in internal politics. If there are domestic constraints limiting French-German cooperation, they arise not from the political system or party alignments of these countries, but from policy priorities: French attachment to an independent defense system, German attachment to the United States as their indispensable security partner, however difficult to live with, and the unwillingness in both countries as well as others in Europe to build the kind of decisionmaking authority (which the European Community, not to mention the Western European Union, manifestly is not) which alone would be capable of developing a credible defense policy based on a common foreign policy. This case shows that, as Le Prestre notes, consensus in France and other countries can inhibit as well as promote policy initiatives that may seem, to many of their citizens as well as others, desirable or even necessary from the point of view of the country's international well-being.

John Mason, in Chapter 3, carries this insight farther into the depths of French politics by explaining the delicate balance developed in the late 1970s between the premises of security policy—above all, an independent nuclear force, a purposely ambiguous doctrine of deterrence governing its prospective engagement, and a "nuclear presidency" to control, symbolize, and validate it (and in part, perhaps, to be validated by it?)—and the political needs of the parties, including, belatedly, the Socialists and even the Communists, which have underlain their consensus on that policy. The consensus is impressive in light of the prior divisions among the French parties on security issues (as is also its extension to nuclear energy development). But its durability for almost a decade now does not guarantee that it will last indefinitely. Mason examines three potential sources of challenge to it:

- Changes in the way France is governed (presidential dominance of policymaking or cohabitation in one or another form) and in the political relations and needs of the parties (in or out of power or sharing it).
- Changes in international circumstances, including superpower arms control negotiations, the Strategic Defense Initiative and its possible sequels, and the problem, which the French have taken very seriously in this decade, of reassuring the nervous West Germans that their well-being can still be best secured within the Western security system (meaning the Atlantic alliance itself but also, insofar as that seems inadequate, supplemental French-German and West European arrangements too), rather than by some flight into neutralism spurred by fear of Soviet power and/or the dream of reunification.
- French development of new nuclear options (and even a non-nuclear one, in the form of the Rapid Action Force (FAR),

valuable, it is hoped, for reassuring the Germans, as well as for use outside Europe) which seem to be at or beyond the margins of the established doctrine of deterrence by means of the threat of the use of nuclear weapons and which may promote debate about whether and how to change that doctrine.

The dual requirement of reassuring the Germans and at the same time making sense of the development and possible deployment of what the French call pre-strategic nuclear weapons with unprecedented capabilities may not be easy to reconcile in a convincing way. Proposals to supplement or replace existing strategic doctrine, if they were not very carefully developed and promptly adopted, might not only trouble the Germans and others whom the French want to reassure but also undermine the established premises of French security itself and confuse or even dissolve the strategic consensus about it that has existed since the late 1970s.

A considerable body of opinion seems to want to manage these complex issues (and obtain financial support to meet defense needs that may become increasingly costly in face, for example, of SDI and possible Soviet responses to it) by "Europeanizing" strategic planning and the uses of French weapons so as to both extend an enhanced French security guarantee to the Federal Republic and give a rational mission to the new kinds of French nuclear weapons at the same time.

But a consensus based on the maintenance and modernization of a nationally controlled nuclear deterrent force has already lost the Communists as policy increasingly emphasizes the deterrence of Soviet aggression against the Federal Republic by increasing cooperation with the allies, including, in the forseeable state of things, the United States. Mason says the French elites may try "drawing closer to NATO in order eventually to move farther away." That would be a subtle and at best very long-term effort. How far can such policies be pushed without facing challenges from elements in the Socialist and Gaullist parties which have already moved a very considerable way in this direction in response to the heightened East-West tensions of the early 1980s (and prevalent anti-Sovietism in French opinion) but may be unwilling to continue much farther, particularly if tension is followed by neo-détente? Some Socialists and Gaullists (not to mention the Communists) may hope to exploit that as an issue in domestic politics as well as in foreign policy in order to reassert, in a less threatening and more fluid international context, France's independence (of the United States) and leadership. In some circumstances, the temptations of French nationalism and of a kind of "neutralism" or "third forcism" which France has scarcely experienced in this decade have a potential for joining forces, if only to challenge new strategies of the kind referred to. For how long can issues of this sort be kept out of debate between, and within, the main non-Communist parties?

Up to now, however, it has been easier for the French leaders and parties (except the Communists) to agree on the need to reassure the Germans and find plausible uses for France's new kinds of nuclear weapons than to work out concrete policies for doing so, whether in a "European" framework or otherwise. As André Brigot says in chapter 4, there has been a striking gap between "emphatic declarations and feeble achievements." There is nothing surprising about this. Brigot shows that the two countries, for all the many interests they have in common, also have deeply different outlooks on the world, rooted in their histories and geographical situations, and therefore have distinctive if not divergent strategic and security concepts. Among these differences are the prevalent attitudes in the two countries concerning the division of Germany, the Soviet threat, the prospect of war in Europe, the role of German territory in such a war, and the planned use of nuclear and conventional weapons to deter or fight it. These are not small differences when it is a question of cooperation on security policy! France's continued economic lag with respect to the Federal Republic, with all that that implies about the French ability to build costly advanced weapon systems, and the stagnation of the German population, with all that that implies for the country's ability to field respectable conventional forces, may seem to make cooperation more imperative but do not make it easier.

Contemplating the ambiguous or contradictory statements of French leaders on these immensely complex subjects, as well as the realities of the situation, I am at least as skeptical as Mason and Brigot that, first, a strategically meaningful European or even French-German defense system can be developed, and, second, that the French parties that claim to agree on the objective are in fact at all agreed on doing the things that would have to be done to attain it. Indeed, they may well be agreed on *not* doing those things. François Mitterrand said in January 1988 that France would not share with anyone its decision to use—or not use—nuclear weapons. Jacques Chirac said that this applies also to prestrategic nuclear weapons. André Giraud said it would be "ridiculous" for anyone to believe that France could cover another part of Europe.

It seems reasonable to take these leaders at their word, as Chancellor Helmut Kohl has in fact done. In that case, "Europeanization" does not seem likely to provide a more coherent doctrine for the use of French nuclear weapons than that now in force. There is, in any case, a risk that this search might, in the meantime, undermine the continued validity of the strategic doctrine on which French security and, even more, the French people's sense of self-confidence have depended for so many years. Preserving that sense while trying to revamp the strategic premises of national defense on which it has been based, thus admitting that they are no longer adequate *before* a new solution is in hand, and calming multiple and self-contradictory German fears at the same time, is an undertaking so daunting that it might well discourage the quest at an early stage, with the result of leaving doctrine still ambiguous, France still free to decide when it will use its nuclear weapons, and the Germans no happier, but perhaps no sadder. It should be noted that the Germans, who are presumably the *demandeurs* in this situation, have received French declarations and initiatives concerning bilateral security cooperation with seeming respect but have made few of their own. Whether they would in fact be much reassured by even the most far-reaching imaginable French commitment to them may be doubted. Whether the problem of reassuring the Germans by military means will remain as important an issue in the coming years as it seems to be now will not be examined here.

In any case, the more serious the discussion becomes in France, the more it is likely to reopen partisan divisions between, and within, the main parties of a kind that has been absent for over a decade. It might even encourage the emergence of antinuclear sentiment from which France, unlike most of its neighbors, has been proudly free precisely because, the French think, they possess nationally controlled nuclear weapons and have a national consensus about their prospective use. On the other hand, can such a debate be avoided in face of superpower actions (whether to develop new weapons or curtail some of those they have, or both)? The answer to these questions, which may have important repercussions on French politics as well as foreign policy, will come from many places besides Paris.

Edward Kolodziej sees opportunities in this developing situation where Mason and Brigot see mainly problems—opportunities not only for France but for the West. In the growing strength of both the French and British nuclear forces, of which he presents the impressive specifics, he finds an increasing capability by these powers both to affect the outbreak and course of hostilities in Europe (something the United States will have to take account of in its management of alliance strategy) and to push the arms control negotiations of the superpowers in directions that could enhance the prospects for disarmament and peace. But the opportunities for bold initiatives which Kolodziej sees opening up as a result of French and British nuclear policies and the likely course of U.S.-Soviet arms control negotiations can be taken advantage of, he believes, only if the United States is willing to concert its negotiating positions and, indeed, share alliance leadership with the two governments in a way it has never done before. Since their nuclear forces have always served political as well as strategic purposes, particularly with respect to their relations with the United States, the French and British are probably ready to bargain, though on conditions not easy to meet. Will the United States be disposed to bargain, to an extent it never has, with them? Can it avoid doing so?

Kolodziej assumes that the Soviet Union will insist on including the French and British forces in a future superpower arms control agreement and that the United States will either have to forego such an agreement or persuade its allies on terms acceptable to them (because it lacks the means to coerce them) to accept cuts or limits in their relatively small forces, even if the agreement fails to meet the conditions they have insisted on if they are to take part: very large reductions in the American and Soviet arsenals. The United States, Kolodziej says, "will have to listen before it will be heard."

That would mean no more disturbing unilateralism, as at Reykjavik. It would mean accepting, at long last, something rather like de Gaulle's 1958 proposal to establish a U.S.-U.K.-French directorate to manage the alliance and other Western interests worldwide.

But would the French welcome this belated U.S. conversion to their initiative, even if it were sweetened by U.S. military assistance? Or might they see it as an embrace that could turn out to be strangling, particularly with respect to their control of their own nuclear weapons, and regard it as inhibiting possible neo-Gaullist diplomatic initiatives that the neo-détente implicit in a superpower strategic arms agreement would presumably offer them? Also, could the Germans be so cavalierly excluded from the highest councils of the alliance, a step which would provocatively—and perhaps dangerously—advertise, as it would presumably be justified by, their non-nuclear status?

Then, the United States would have to assure the allies of the reliability of its guarantee to them, stopping (or precluding) what many in Europe see as a drift to decoupling. But how far can it or any country go in trying to absolutely assure another that it will certainly do some given thing in the future? Can it reassure the allies any more convincingly than it is doing now or has done for most of the last forty years: never so well as to entirely satisfy them but never so inadequately as to provoke them to seek a more nearly satisfactory security system or, as they have noticed, to induce a Soviet attack on any of them? U.S. policymakers would also have to give up (if they hold) the dream of somehow securing strategic superiority over the Soviet Union. That might mean renunciation of SDI as it has been presented, which in any case would have to be part of the intra-alliance as well as the East-West bargaining that Kolodziej envisages because it threatens in the long run the effectiveness and credibility of the French and British nuclear forces.

Kolodziej recognizes the difficulties that lie in the way of implementing his proposals but thinks the alliance is faced with such threats of decomposition, enhanced by the new vigor of Soviet diplomacy, as to require the members to make the necessary efforts. The benefits he sees, however, would not be limited to damage control within the alliance. Interesting opportunities for French-British strategic cooperation would open up, with further prospects for expanding that to the West European level and eventually reducing if not eliminating the security dependence of the area on the United States. As Western Europeans, and particularly West Germans, came to feel more confident about their security situation and their role in it, they would be in a position to contribute to an even more dramatic change in the international constellation: "a gradual shift in emphasis from nuclear and conventional deterrence to socioeconomic and political competition between East and West." Changes underway in the Soviet Union, and the internal weaknesses that underlie them, give us reason, in Kolodziej's view, to think such a shift might now be in the realm of possibility. (But would the Russians be willing to shift the main form of competition to an area in which, however much they may restructure their economy, they will be in a decidedly inferior position for a long time?) It is for the Western allies to so order their security and other relations as to be able to take advantage of the opportunities now emerging.

This prospect of fundamentally rebuilding the post-1945 international system will seem challenging to some, visionary to others. Kolodziej may be right to think that the French-British and West European common action with respect to defense, which he believes desirable or even necessary if superpower arms control agreements are to be achieved, cannot be arrived at solely in the framework of negotiations limited to those issues but requires a bolder set of objectives to help the Europeans overcome the deeply rooted obstacles to security cooperation among themselves and to their participation in arms control. But is such common action, however desirable it may seem for these and other reasons, going to be more feasible in the oncoming circumstances Kolodziej foresees, or others, than it has proved to be in seemingly favorable conditions in the past? If not, must the superpowers give up all hope of agreement on strategic arms limitations or reductions?

Many things that have seemed "obvious" and "necessary"—including greater West European cooperation for defense—have failed over long years to be realized in face of obstacles that have stood, and continue to stand, in the way. Will it be different now? Are the opportunities for improving East-West relations so great as to break down these obstacles? Are they, on the other hand, limited to this one path? Are the challenges to maintaining an adequate degree of intra-alliance cooperation so uniquely urgent as to lead all right-thinking people in the direction indicated? Certainly, a remarkable level of statesmanship would be required on all sides, as well as concurrent trends in the United States, the Soviet Union, and the West European countries. But such a level of skill, or even a somewhat lower level, might find ways to promote arms control and resist alliance decay by means other than these.

The skeptics among us are likely to remain skeptical about the realization of such ambitious projects. Yet, even if bold new policies do not emerge, consideration of them might at least enlighten us about why more modest efforts to the same ends need to be, and can be, pursued.

The 1988 French presidential election was not, as some people expected, the occasion for a "great debate" among the candidates about the future of the country's foreign and defense policies. The voters seem to have cast their ballots, as usual, on the basis of economic and social issues, partisan loyalties and the perceived qualities of the candidates. François Mitterrand and the ministers he appoints, however, will have to give serious attention to the needs and options of French policy as discussed in the chapters that follow and then make some important decisions. These decisions, in turn, whatever the mix in them of perseverance and innovation, will both reflect and affect not only France's foreign and security policies but its internal politics, in a period when politics promises to be remarkably "interesting."

CHAPTER 2

The Lessons of Cohabitation

PHILIPPE G. LE PRESTRE

At the very moment political pundits were praising the "normalization" of French politics in the mid-1980s (illustrated by the decline of ideology, alternation between two major parties, or coalitions, pragmatism, and governmental stability), uncertainty came back with a vengeance in the form first of cohabitation in 1986-1988, then of President Mitterrand's reelection in May 1988 followed by the election of a legislature without a socialist or conservative majority.

What factors are likely to influence the future course of French foreign and security policies? Although various explanations of French behavior have been advanced, few studies have sought systematically to test them. Rather, the experience of the Fifth Republic and the Gaullist record have been considered so unique that, apart from attempts to uncover continuities and discontinuities between the Fourth and Fifth Republics, longitudinal studies have been neglected. Explanations do abound, but they are limited to a single policymaker rather than applied to several of them in order to identify a pattern. For example, systemic variables may have defined the foreign policy problématique of de Gaulle, domestic requirements that of Pompidou.[1] Giscard d'Estaing favored a peace-through-trade approach whereas Mitterrand followed de Gaulle in the belief that power must be balanced. But recent work on the decisionmaking process has compared several presidents within this common institutional framework and augurs well for a fruitful application of concepts drawn from the comparative study of foreign policy.[2]

The dominance of de Gaulle and the nature of the institutions he bequeathed the country encouraged explanations based on individual variables. Outputs resulted from the leader's intelligence of the situation and corresponded to a rationally determined course of action in pursuit of clear and consistent goals. Psychological explanations were overlooked—especially regarding de Gaulle's successors—and domestic factors considered only on an ad hoc basis. The dominance of the president supposedly minimized the importance of bureaucratic variables. Indeed, the Gaullist record seemed to indicate that a country could largely free itself from domestic and systemic constraints, or at least that the latter did not determine behavior. By contrast, domestic political forces were thought to have often played a crucial role in defining French foreign policy during the Fourth Republic.[3] Regime variables have therefore figured prominently in explanations both of the process and of the content of the policy. Can the hitherto unique situation of 1986–1988 known as "cohabitation" help us evaluate the many factors affecting French security policy and, in particular, assess the relative importance of the nature of the regime? What clues can it provide as to the future course of that policy?

The Advent of Cohabitation

On 23 March 1986, to a mixture of horror and fascination, the French political class rediscovered a situation thought to have disappeared with the Third Republic. After years of expectation, the country finally entered a period of cohabitation when Prime Minister Chirac presented his coalition cabinet to President Mitterrand, a Socialist. Whatever their opinion about its virtue and viability, the French have been fond of referring to this situation as an "experiment." It was to test the institutions of the Fifth Republic (would they still enable efficient and responsive government?), the political class (would they know how to play the game?), and the political culture (would the French accept it?).

Calling this situation an experiment suggested that its outcome was uncertain, but identifiable, and that one would gain greater knowledge about the nature of French politics. This period indeed provides a unique opportunity for examining the nature of French foreign policymaking and the various explanations that coexist in foreign policy analysis. Cohabitation seems particularly well-suited for testing regime-based—or institutional—explanations.

Cohabitation was born after the 16 March 1986 legislative elections had given a narrow majority to a coalition of the neo-Gaullist Rally for the Republic (RPR), headed by Jacques Chirac, and of the center-right Union for French Democracy (UDF), itself a coalition of four parties. Since President Mitterrand chose not to follow the "advice" of prominent members of the new majority to resign, France entered a new era of political uncertainty. Uncertainty was particularly acute in foreign policy. Although President Mitterrand had largely continued his predecessors' policies or returned more prominently to Gaullist orthodoxy, Jacques Chirac had repeatedly criticized the Socialists' foreign policy—from its third-worldism and support for the admission of Spain and Portugal to the European Community, to its rejection of the Strategic Defense Initiative, and its defense priorities. Yet, the heir to the Gaullist movement, a former prime minister of Giscard d'Estaing, and a man with little foreign policy experience, was now to share in the president's traditional *domaine réservé*. The major change was therefore institutional: foreign policy would be defined and conducted both by the president and the prime minister. What did this entail for the process and the content of the policy?

The greatest uncertainties concerned the distribution of power between the president and the prime minister. The constitution of 1958 instituted a dyarchy in foreign policy, whereas its political practice has sanctioned the dominance of the president. Articles 5, 14, 15, 16, 52, and the 1964 decree on the employment of nuclear forces give the president broad powers to define and oversee foreign and defense policies. Articles 20, 21, and 53 entrust the prime minister with the determination and direction of foreign policy. Together with a hold on the bureaucracy, these prerogatives give the prime minister greater discretionary powers. Yet, the traditional presidential interpretation distinguishes between the conceptual, impelling, and political role of the president on the one hand, from the management and implementation function of the prime minister on the other. De Gaulle's successors, including Mitterrand, went even further. As then-President Giscard d'Estaing emphasized: ". . . in our Republic, in addition to the president who is in charge of permanent and essential matters, the executive includes a prime minister who handles contingent problems."[4] According to this conception, the prime minister manages daily economic, administrative, political, and legislative matters. What the government conceives is left up to the president's discretion because he is "the supreme judge of the national interest" and the source of all power.[5] But this interpretation becomes more questionable when the prime minister can claim a separate legitimacy and is responsible to a legislature whose majority coalition does not support the president.

"A constitution," de Gaulle once said, "is a spirit, institutions, and a practice."[6] The problem, at the onset of cohabitation, did not concern the protocol and administrative functions that Matignon (the residence of the prime minister) traditionally performs (the foreign affairs budget, various financial helps and special funds, trips and meetings with other heads of government). Rather, it lay in who was to define policy, how the responses and reactions to sudden events were to be developed, and who would direct secret diplomacy and oversee nominations.[7]

Regimes and Foreign Policy

"Regime" commonly designates the existing institutions and the political personnel in power. One can contrast the "Old" with the "Republican" regime, identify various constitutional regimes (the Fourth versus the Fifth Republic), or simply speak of the Gaullist, Giscardian, and Mitterrand regimes. I shall retain and expand Barbara and Stephen Salmore's specific usage here. A "regime" will refer to "authoritative political leadership," that is, to the pattern of allocation of state power. Regimes may change while the basic political structure remains.[8] What matters is the distribution of power among existing institutions and the rules of the game. Thus, since the 1958 constitution lends itself to two interpretations (one favoring the president, the other the prime minister), two different regimes are possible.

An examination of this variable led the Salmores to speculate that differences in regimes should explain differences in foreign policy behavior, with the nature of these differences stemming from the leaders' foremost need to maximize their political support. What matters is not who is in power, but how power is allocated and whose interests are represented among the leadership.

A change of regime modifies the array and nature of constraints that policymakers must face. These constraints can be political or pertain to the availability of key resources, such as control of civil society (the economy, natural resources, public opinion), the regime's degree of political institutionalization (its autonomy from civil society, the efficiency of the bureaucracy, established decisonmaking processes), and its level of public support. Political constraints include the degree of unity of the regime, the nature and extent of regime accountability (political participation and competition), and the degree to which the regime represents the wider society.[9]

Clearly, cohabitation signified a change of regime in addition to amplifying other trends toward an apparent "normalization." Both the distribution of power and the rules of the game changed. Decisionmaking power was now shared. Although the nationalization of banks and major industries had increased the Socialist government's control of the economy, control over public opinion diminished after 1985, thanks to several radio and television reforms. The bureaucracy has been accused of becoming increasingly politicized since the late 1960s, losing its effectiveness and reliability. The return of the conservative parties in 1986 renewed attempts to replace prominent socialist appointees with supporters of the new majority, which led to clashes not only with the president but also among the partners of the winning coalition. Yet, replacements after 16 March 1986 were few because of the "watchfulness" of the president, so that many "socialist" appointees coexisted with partisans of the new majority. The turnover in the Ministry of Foreign Affairs was limited to a few ambassadors whose nomination had been resented by career foreign service officers.

Public opinion acted as a powerful constraint in several ways. On the one hand, its support for the two leaders was obviously divided: each had his own constituency, although each tried to woo the center. On the other hand, the constitution of the Fifth Republic had wide support, and so did the idea of cohabitation. One could therefore easily submit that cohabitation created a regime that was operating under much greater constraints than any other since the advent of the Fifth Republic. This development, in turn should have definite foreign policy implications.

Six Hypotheses

Presidential dominance has traditionally been regarded as holding several benefits for French foreign policy. First comes the ability to make clear choices and reach quick decisions, but also to develop long-term initiatives in relative secrecy. Naturally, this ability is tempered by individual idiosyncracies. Giscard d'Estaing lacked the strategic understanding of de Gaulle who himself was rather oblivious to the importance of economic factors other than as power resources. Although Giscard d'Estaing seemed to control more of the details of foreign policy than did de Gaulle, he was forceful and able to impose his decisions only when he felt knowledgeable about the topic or when he held a clear interest in the issue.[10]

Consistency is also supposed to be the hallmark of presidential dominance. A renewable seven-year mandate enables the president to develop and pursue initiatives that may take time to bear fruit. His autonomy also allows the pursuit of policies in the face of strong opposition until their benefits become clear or until it proves impossible to question them. A weakened National Assembly, with little control over the foreign affairs budget, little information about issues and executive actions, and restricted foreign policy debates, ensures that long-term goals are pursued unimpeded by volatile majorities or immediate domestic political considerations.

According to this perspective, bureaucratic variables play a more secondary role in determining outputs. Bureaucratic conflicts are certainly present,[11] but foreign policy is not the result of compromises among competing agencies. The president sets a clear direction and arbitrates effectively among the various positions presented to him.

Presidential dominance therefore generates policies that largely reflect individual preferences. De Gaulle's policies, both in style and content, mirrored his experiences and prejudices. Once in charge, the true character of the individual is revealed. Jacques Chirac and his advisers, for example, expected Giscard d'Estaing to be self-effaced in 1974. Yet, Giscard proved to be very directive, to the great discomfort of his prime minister.[12]

Finally, as noted earlier, domestic political considerations have less influence upon foreign policy, a development clearly seen in the transition between the Fourth and the Fifth Republic. Apart from having greater freedom to ignore domestic pressures, governments are not as dependent upon immediate successes. Parliamentary regimes cannot take many risks, for the rules of the game often dictate the resignation of the responsible government in case of failure. The domestic impact of foreign policy therefore minimizes surprises and forceful actions, and hinders coherence and consistency in the definition and pursuit of long-term objectives.

Applying the regime approach to French cohabitation, one would expect that clientelism and domestic considerations would become more significant in foreign policymaking. If "a regime's primary goal is to maximize its political support" in order to remain in power,[13] then the period of cohabitation should reflect each leader's concern with conducting a foreign policy that would, in his mind, generate the largest electoral payoffs. Foreign policy becomes hostage to domestic politics.

This proposition leads to three hypotheses. First, the foreign policy style of each leader should reflect his respective electoral concerns (H1). Second, the content of the policy should reflect domestic priorities (H2). Jacques Chirac who, as a protégé of

President Pompidou, shared his mentor's belief in the primacy of domestic politics, would be expected to utilize his large powers for the benefit of key domestic groups in preparation for the 1988 presidential elections. In particular, his government would make specific efforts to implement the foreign policy propositions included in the joint RPR-UDF electoral platform drafted before the 1986 legislative elections. Third, a weakened state would be less able to pursue an independent foreign policy (H3). The state's capacity to transform the international system is reduced because it is unable to use its available resources effectively or marshall the necessary ones.[14]

Reasoning a contrario from the characteristics of presidential dominance, one would also expect that (H4) foreign policy outputs will increasingly reflect bureaucratic conflicts, and (H5) tend toward less consistency.[15] Finally, inertia or worse, stalemate will characterize cohabitation (H6). Highly constrained regimes will have a reduced foreign policy activity and will demonstrate "lower levels of commitment" than less constrained regimes.[16] This belief was widely held before the 1986 elections. Chaos or paralysis would arise from overlapping foreign policy prerogatives. Decisionmaking would be arduous, and implementation slow and hazardous. Less pessimistic observers, or those with fewer political motives, argued that inertia would most likely characterize cohabitation, with dire consequences for French leadership in Europe and in the Third World. Resting on a factional base, a government of cohabitation would avoid contentious positions and confine its activity to reacting to the behavior of others rather than formulating new initiatives or implementing a concerted policy of its own.[17]

What is important is not whether phenomena that these hypotheses describe are present, but whether they are present to a higher degree compared to the preceding regime. With this in mind, let us now turn to the record of cohabitation. To assess the validity of these six hypotheses, we shall concentrate on two prominent policy areas: defense and Europe—two overlapping domains over which Mitterrand insisted on exercising close leadership.[18]

Cohabitation and Defense

One of the most spectacular events of President Mitterrand's 1981-1986 foreign policy record was advocacy of positions that he had widely opposed in the past, or that were utterly unexpected. This evolution led to a kind of schizophrenic policy that unsettled many party members and largely disarmed the opposition.[19] On the one hand, the president took up traditional socialist themes regarding the Third World and human rights, and used foreign policy to ensure the success of domestic policies. On the other hand, he conducted a Gaullist policy based on independent nuclear forces and decisionmaking, and on the importance of power relationships. One spectacular manifestation of this attitude was the strong support given the deployment of INF missiles in 1983 before the *Bundestag*. A dramatic illustration of the resulting apparent consensus was the broad approval of the 1987-1991 Military Planning Law, which only the members of the Communist party—and one Socialist deputy— opposed. For the first time, all the major parties had supported a Military Planning Law. Although Mitterrand's endorsement made it difficult for the Socialists to vote against it—as they had the foreign affairs budget that previous October—they could conceivably have abstained, yet did not.

Although there was general agreement among the major political parties over the principles that should govern the defense of the country, uncertainty and controversies regarding doctrinal questions remained. How could France deter an attack against Germany, securely help tie German public opinion to the Atlantic alliance, and alleviate German fears of nuclear war, while maintaining its autonomy of decision regarding the use of its weapons? Should it make explicit commitments or retain an ambiguous position? Should it guarantee Germany's security? If so, where? Should battlefield nuclear weapons and nuclear artillery be considered "tactical" (that is, usable as any other conventional weapon system), "pre-strategic" (that is, signifying a change of character in the conflict and a warning that strategic systems will be used), or simply eliminated? How should be solved the trade-off between modernizing nuclear forces (so as to prevent any war in Europe) and improving conventional forces (to defend global French interests and meet German wishes)?

Between 1981 and 1986, the Socialists attempted to resolve these questions by actively supporting the deployment of Pershing II and cruise missiles—whereas Giscard d'Estaing had claimed it was of no concern to the French—by creating a Rapid Action Force (FAR) to be used in the early phases of a conflict in Germany, and by labeling battlefield nuclear weapons "pre-strategic," thus rejecting the idea of limited nuclear war-fighting capability that the Reagan administration was pursuing at the time. Mitterrand criticized the Strategic Defense Initiative (SDI) and, with the Eureka project, sought to organize and strengthen European research capacities in order to preclude a U.S. takeover of the most advanced sectors of Europe's technology industry. In October 1986, Mitterrand reiterated the principles on which he thought the configuration of French defense should be based: (1) short-range nuclear weapons are first of all ultimate warnings, not part of a nuclear battlefield or elements of a flexible response; (2) priority is given to the modernization of the strategic submarine forces; and (3) the new ICBM (the SX) will be based in existing fixed silos (instead of being mobile).[20] All these "principles" were opposed by most members of the new majority coalition.

Given the evolution of the Socialist party (described by John Mason in chapter 3 of this book), Mitterrand's record, and divergent views within and between the UDF and the RPR, the joint 1986 electoral platform of the conservative parties remained vague on defense and foreign policy. They pledged to increase the military budget to about 4 percent of GDP, to diversify nuclear forces, to develop a common position on the SDI with Britain and Germany, to modernize conventional defense, to develop with Britain and Germany a doctrine governing the use of nuclear weapons, and to reinforce relations with traditional African partners.

The UDF endorsed the "tactical" nature of battlefield nuclear weapons, pressed for the manufacture and deployment of the neutron bomb, and urged closer cooperation with NATO. Jacques Chirac supported the dual-track approach and also sought to anchor France more firmly into a common NATO defensive strategy, a position that went further than several of the old Gaullist "barons" would have liked. He pledged to pursue the development of the mobile missile that the Socialist government had put on hold, and to manufacture and deploy the neutron bomb.[21] Along with Giscard d'Estaing, he endorsed SDI and the U.S. call for European participation. Regarding the question of the defense of France's neighbors, Chirac remained ambiguous. On the one hand, he believed that France could not extend a unilateral pledge of nuclear security guarantees to the German Federal Republic, for France had to retain its independence of decision. On the other hand, he believed that early participation in a conflict was inevitable and might require the use of "tactical" nuclear weapons separately from strategic ones, a possibility that both Mitterrand and the Germans have opposed.[22] His speeches pointed to greater integration of French defense into NATO's plans, reaffirming that France's security started on the Elbe.

Despite these differences, agreement on the Planning Law was easily reached. Focusing only on equipment expenditures, the Law sought to reach the threshold of 4 percent of GNP in five years. No major program was abandoned. The Rapid Action Force remained in existence and the "pre-strategic function" of battlefield nuclear weapons was reaffirmed. The trade-off between developing a mobile replacement for the old ICBMs (a project supported by the Defense ministry) and modernizing the nuclear strategic force was solved to the benefit of the latter with the pursuit of the current SLBM retrofitting program, the construction of a sixth nuclear submarine, and the planned development of a new SLBM (the M5). Mitterrand was not willing to postpone the modernization of the sea-based deterrent, which he considered a more reliable component of France's future deterrent posture. Indeed, the Planning Law again favored nuclear over conventional forces, despite earlier conservative criticisms. Two other initiatives were also noteworthy: the neutron bomb was to be manufactured and deployed (although German hostility may limit that possibility) and the decision was made to develop and manufacture new chemical weapons.

Agreement was possible largely because these choices did not seem irreversible, or the Planning Law contained projects that each leader supported. For example, the key to the "tactical" or "pre-strategic" character of battlefield nuclear weapons lies in their deployment. Will they be gathered into a single division directly under the president's orders, or will they be decentralized to each corps, giving commanders the capacity to use them in support of conventional operations? The multiple tensions between conventional and nuclear weapons, between modernization and maintenance, and between forces designed to deter a soviet attack and those designed to protect French interests abroad, remain. Responding to broad criticisms within the military that the RPR had echoed before 1986, the Law planned for conventional programs. The development and construction of a new aircraft carrier was to be pursued, AWACS and satellites—which the Chadian experience showed were sorely needed—purchased, and a new tank and new fighter aircraft developed. Yet, there were no specific commitments for each program and future economic constraints may prove important. The operating budget was also unknown. It is therefore likely that conventional forces will again be short-changed.

One way to overcome financial constraints is through greater European technical and strategic cooperation. Italy is to participate in the development of the Helios military observation satellite, but the United Kingdom remained largely deaf to French proposals. An agreement to develop jointly a new fighter helicopter after more than ten years of negotiations was finally reached with Germany in

July 1987. Thus, the search for a defense formula with the Federal Republic not only responded to widespread fears of a German drift toward neutrality, but also sprung from the difficulties of maintaining an independent French force. Hesitations and controversies within Germany, suspicions in Britain, and divisions within the RPR have rendered the pursuit of this task difficult.

The October 1986 Reykjavik summit and Secretary Gorbachev's proposals of the following March provided another test of the regime of cohabitation. Was there a consensus over the analysis of these events and the proper responses with which to greet them, or incoherence and conflict between the two men? Did it lead to major French initiatives, to a reconsideration of traditional policy, or to a reaffirmation of the latter?

Rather than a simple vicissitude of East-West relations, the Reykjavik summit has in fact acquired the same symbolic importance as the Suez crisis of thirty years earlier which had an enormous impact on French and British foreign policies.[23] Reykjavik catalyzed mounting concerns about the reliability of the U.S. nuclear guarantee. The apparent readiness to enter into a deal with the Soviet Union that would further the U.S. national interest in limiting the danger of nuclear escalation and mobilize domestic support, while ignoring the fears of its European allies, demonstrated the uncertainty of the U.S. commitments. Yet, although shaken, European policy elites still derived different implications from these events. Some sought closer cooperation with the United States in the hope of influencing the negotiations, others became convinced that salvation lay in the development of a powerful European defense, and still others were attracted by the prospect of a denuclearized Europe, or even neutrality. Most believed that preventing a U.S. drift toward isolationism was imperative, whether one viewed a future Europe as an adjunct to U.S. power, or as an independent force. The French and British wondered how they could influence the negotiations between the superpowers without becoming an indirect party to them.

But European silence fell on the Reykjavik summit. The first reactions of the French government were muted. The strategic and alliance implications of what had happened were ominously clear, yet European public opinion would have hardly understood outright glee. Chirac said only that he was "not as pessimistic as others."[24] The first lengthy reaction came from Jean-Bernard Raimond, the minister of Foreign Affairs. France, he said, "fears the prospect of the total elimination of American nuclear weapons in Europe,"[25] which would weaken both the Atlantic alliance and Europe, expose the

French and British nuclear forces to greater Soviet and U.S. pressures, and leave imbalances in short-range nuclear missiles and conventional forces untouched. This position reflected the need not just to deter nuclear war, but to prevent any war.

A certain hesitation characterized the French position, caught between the negative implications of the summit, the traditional position that France is not concerned by other countries' disarmament negotiations,[26] and the need to spare public opinion. Soon after the summit, Mitterrand went to London to talk with Prime Minister Thatcher and reaffirm France's wish not to be included in the negotiations (which she hurriedly conveyed to President Reagan in person). Yet, France's own analyses and previous behavior belied this professed lack of interest. Mitterrand himself had made it France's interest in 1983 to be involved in the dual-track proposal and to support the deployment of INFs.

The following December, Jacques Chirac submitted the text of a European Defense Charter to the members of the Western European Union intended to appease the partisans of greater European cooperation, rally other governments around a common position, and, above all, reinforce the legitimacy of the French nuclear deterrent.[27] Yet, France did not take the lead in forcefully and publicly articulating a European position, whereas it had not hesitated to do so on numerous occasions in the past (although France's absence from NATO's integrated military command makes this role difficult). Ironically, Britain now assumed this traditional French role and became a privileged interlocutor of both superpowers during the subsequent INF negotiations.

Divergences within the French government arose in response to Secretary Gorbachev's acceptance of the zero-option in February 1987.[28] But they came from relatively unexpected quarters. Cohabitation has led to a certain tendency to preempt the foreign policy debate and present the other party with a *fait accompli.* The Quai d'Orsay released a dismissive communiqué soon after the announcement. This, in turn, prompted a public rebuff from the president, more for procedural than substantive reasons, because the communiqué reiterated the traditional French position that both Mitterrand in 1981 and Raimond in 1986 had reaffirmed. But the ministry apparently failed to clear it with the Elysée, which feared that its negative tone would puzzle the electorate and isolate France from her alliance partners.

Reflecting the opinion of the military, André Giraud, the Defense minister, rejected the Soviet offer outright, calling its acceptance, "a European Munich."[29] His position had wide support among hard-line

Gaullists as well as within the foreign policy community. Mitterrand however chose to correct him with the support of Chirac. Although the latter favored outright rejection, he quickly supported Mitterrand's more moderate approach. Preferring a less dramatic style, Mitterrand wished to show that France was not a priori hostile to arms reduction. He considered crucial the battles for French and German public opinions, and found it politically difficult to reject something the West had been asking.

The French position, in principle favorable to the opening of negotiations, was subsequently articulated almost exclusively by the president. But his concern for various public opinions within and outside France tended to confuse his discourse. He refrained from imposing conditions for French support of this process—arguing that France could not both wish to influence the negotiations and claim not to be affected by them. Several points contradicted his earlier stands and his approval of the December Charter proposal, as well as the Gaullist analyses he had previously championed. Whereas his prime minister sought to ward off a possible American withdrawal, Mitterrand was not "particularly troubled" by a possible decoupling: "Deterrence remains intact since strategic systems are not included. . . . The American commitment to Europe does not necessarily lie in the presence of euromissiles. There is an alliance."[30] A common destiny and strategic interest would form the basis of a U.S. guarantee. Yet, a month later, in agreement with the United Kingdom, the French insisted on the inclusion of short-range missiles in the negotiations, and on the need to "couple" European and U.S. security. As Jacques Chirac exclaimed during the debate on the Military Planning Law:

> The threat on our existence caused by the existence of the nuclear, conventional and chemical soviet arsenal, will continue justifying on our part an important defense effort. . . . [S]o long as the bloated arsenals of the superpowers and the imbalances in conventional forces in Europe remain, France's security will demand nuclear deterrence. . . .The zero-option would have negative and dangerous consequences if it appeared to public opinion as foreshadowing an inevitable American withdrawal and, above all, the denuclearization of Europe. It would mean, however, an opportunity for our country and for its allies if it provided the opportunity for all to realize the security requirements of our continent through the maintenance of a credible nuclear deterrent, close ties between Western Europe and the United States, and through a greater European commitment to its own defense.[31]

Other features of French security policy went unquestioned. Cooperation with the Federal Republic took on more dramatic and symbolic aspects with the June 1987 decision to set up a joint brigade (as suggested by Chancellor Kohl), with Mitterrand's proposal the following September of a joint defense council, and with the staging of special military maneuvers (code-named "Bold Sparrow") that demonstrated France's willingness and capacity to come to the rapid aid of Germany with its FAR.

Both Mitterrand and Chirac reaffirmed the need for the superpowers to concentrate their disarmament efforts globally on strategic forces, and, in Europe, on conventional ones. But there again, signals to allies differed. Whereas Mitterrand would apparently prefer outright elimination of theater weapons (especially as part of a deal on conventional weapons), which he considers useless if not dangerous, Chirac and most of the RPR-UDF still value them.

Thus, inconsistencies or hesitancy, mentioned earlier in reference to Reykjavik, were present elsewhere and theatened French credibility (admittedly not a uniquely French or cohabitationist trait but one that cohabitation accentuated). One protagonist would advance an idea or try to present the other with a *fait accompli*, the other would respond a few days later. Yet, these attempts were usually settled to the president's advantage. Whether it was SDI, the role of theater nuclear weapons, the responses to Reykjavik and to the INF treaty, budgetary priorities, or the modernization of short-range nuclear weapons, Chirac chose not to challenge the president further, often against the feelings of his own majority.

For example, in September 1986, Chirac, following his party platform, clearly separated strategic and theater nuclear weapons, a distinction Mitterrand rejects. Thus, Chirac spoke of the need for a new short-range mobile missile. Placing himself squarely within a strategy of flexible response, the prime minister referred to a graduated series of warnings that such a weapon could provide. Soon thereafter, the president reaffirmed the strategic function of theater weapons. He publicly reiterated his condemnation of flexible response in February 1988 in Dublin where he voiced his opposition to the modernization of short-range nuclear weapons favored by the British prime minister. This last example illustrates Mitterrand's keen appreciation of the political dimension of the security debate which underlay his reaction to Reykjavik and to the INF treaty and which includes the preservation of a nuclear consensus at home and the prevention of growing pacifist or neutralist sentiments in West Germany.

Cohabitation and Europe

The domestic implications of defense issues are largely restricted to the armed forces, to the armament industry, and to a few specialized observers as long as the pacifist movement remains weak and public debate is limited. European issues, however, are intertwined with domestic ones. One would then expect a sharp manifestation of the developments hypothesized in regime-based explanations.

Along with the UDF, François Mitterrand has been a vocal advocate of greater European cooperation and integration. He first sought to use Europe to consolidate domestic reforms, then worked out a temporary solution to the budgetary controversies raised by Margaret Thatcher. Numerous proposals were made—most of which withered away—yet a few gained momentum. France launched the Eureka project and urged greater technological cooperation. Above all, by developing close rapport with Helmut Kohl, Mitterrand continued the close relationship that Giscard d'Estaing had enjoyed with Helmut Schmidt. Both sought to revive the defense clause of the 1963 Franco-German treaty and give more substance to the moribund Western European Union—to some American displeasure. Finally, Mitterrand actively promoted the 1985 "Single European Act" that reformed the European Community's decisionmaking procedures and sought yet again to create a European market—the initial objectives of the Treaty of Rome—this time by the end of 1992, and formalized the existing scope of the Community's activities. All these initiatives were not only rooted in a genuine European consciousness, but also in his concern about German neutralist propensities, in the growing divergence of U.S. and European interests, and in the belief that the success of domestic reforms could be found abroad. Yet, this commitment was less evident in foreign relations: France did not bother to strengthen the fledgling European political cooperation nor to consult with its partners on several occasions, which marked a move backward from Giscard's efforts.[32]

The RPR has always supported cooperation while strongly rejecting integration. In 1978, Chirac campaigned against the election of the European parliament by universal suffrage. Mostly equating European construction with the Commmon Agricultural Program (CAP), he opposed the admission of Portugal and Spain into the European Community in 1986 which he vowed to reexamine if elected, and he ignored the other industrial, technological, and political aspects of the Community. It was clear that Europe would be dismissed as an enterprise worthy in itself, rather than as a way of gaining advantages for France.

Europe was indeed neglected after March 1986. Initiatives withered. No proposals were made to find new resources, reform the CAP, or develop a vision for the Europe of the 1990s that would transcend its mercantile aspects. Monetary union and collaboration in other areas, such as foreign policy and human rights, were neglected. Some of this is linked to the reported poor relations that have developed between Jacques Chirac and Helmut Kohl. The chancellor clearly favored his relationship with Mitterrand; Chirac was either unable or unwilling to develop closer ties.[33] At the same time, the Federal Republic's European commitment dwindled.

Two episodes epitomized this lack of enthusiasm. First, the nomination of an undersecretary of state for European Affairs was delayed until six months into Chirac's tenure (although initial reports in March 1986 suggested that Mitterrand wanted to leave it open for a while). Second, the government's attitude toward the "Single European Act," signed in February 1986 on the eve of the legislative elections, was rather lukewarm. After some hesitations during the spring and summer of 1986, the government precipitously submitted it for ratification in the fall, only to postpone it until late in the session. This attitude caused sharp conflicts within the majority coalition. At least one UDF minister threatened to resign if the treaty were not sent to Parliament, which finally ratified it a few weeks short of the 31 December deadline. Jean-Bernard Raimond's first point in support of ratification was emblematic of the misgivings of the RPR and of the Foreign ministry: "First of all," he told deputies, "this ratification seems inevitable to me insofar as the Single Act would not justify a European crisis provoked by France."[34] This made the UDF very suspicious of the prime minister's commitment. During the same debate, Giscard d'Estaing even exclaimed: "We shall ask that you have the political will to abide by the December 31st, 1992 deadline. In this respect, we shall ask that you do not propose—and I will tell you that we are ready not to approve—anything that would go against it."[35]

Never a European enthusiast, Chirac was caught between the anti-European attitude of old hard-line Gaullists, the UDF partisans of greater integration, and a president eager to maintain the achievements of recent years. Thus, opposition to European construction did not materialize in the dramatic denunciation of past agreements or in the interruption of previous programs such as Eureka. A motion to constitute a special parliamentary commission to investigate the impact of the admission of Spain and Portugal into the Community was passed, then quietly withdrawn. Rather, opposition came in the form of delays, lack of interest, absence, inertia, and lukewarm implementation.

Early tensions between the two leaders concerned the replacement of Socialist appointees. Mitterrand reportedly would not agree to the eviction of the head of the interministerial coordination committee for European economic cooperation.[36] Choosing not to make it a matter of principle, Chirac in effect bypassed her. Although she remained to keep the president informed—a key concern since he only has a small staff—her influence greatly diminished. The French representative to the European Community also found himself in the same position. Despite the nomination of two former Socialist ministers to the European commission (Jacques Delors at its head, and Claude Cheysson back as a commissioner), Mitterrand's capacities to influence France's European policy were greatly diminished. This situation eventually made the support for the nomination of an undersecretary more worthwhile, which Chirac then delayed for several months.

Although Mitterrand has favored a reform of the CAP, while Chirac, in the Gaullist tradition that sees Europe as little else than a means for supporting French agriculture, opposed it, both defended price supports and direct aid to farmers, as well as an increase in the Community's resources. Despite some positioning for self-advantage and electoral appeal, both worked in tandem in June 1987 to help engineer an agreement on agricultural prices. Thus, although their respective visions may have differed, their proximate goals and tactics coincided and allowed for cooperation. European summits in fact saw a division of labor of sorts. At the June 1987 summit, Chirac concentrated on agricultural prices (the short term), Mitterrand on the common agricultural policy (the long term). A few contradictions and haphazard behavior were evident, yet a compromise was reached with other partners without apparent acrimony within the French camp.

Despite this modus vivendi, the president could do little to promote greater activism. He traveled extensively, kept in close contact with European leaders, and often lobbied the French government from abroad. Appealing to public opinion, his speeches urged bold moves and called for "a Europe with centralized political authority" which would be able to make its own decisions about "the means of its security."[37]

The nomination as minister for Agriculture of the head of a powerful farm union indicated the new government's desire to cultivate the support of the farmers, which it had courted in previous years. Subsidies were approved in violation of the government's self-imposed budgetary constraints. The defense of the French farmer—a tradition the Socialist governments had eagerly espoused—did cause some problems in the relations between the two men now that the president had adopted a loftier perspective. Chirac was not eager to side with Mitterrand against his minister for Agriculture.

The Impact of Regime Change

We now can return to our six hypotheses in light of these two cases. First, did the style of French foreign policy reflect greater concern for the domestic audience (H1)? Ministers adopted attitudes that had strong electoral overtones, especially on European issues. After all, one does not want to be accused of negotiating the French farmers away. But that is common to every government. Stripped of much of his power, Mitterrand cast himself as a Father of the Nation, a symbol of continuity, seemingly above electoral politics, watching over the prime minister's activities while looking toward the future and a greater role for France. Each had strong incentives to use foreign policy for electoral gain, so clashes were inevitable. For example, Chirac's attempt to claim credit for the Franco-Spanish rapprochement drew a sharp rebuff by Mitterrand.[38] Rather than promoting grandstanding, cohabitation affected style negatively. Dramatic gestures were less common for fear that they would lead to a feeling of being upstaged on the part of the other leader. France, which had equated foreign policy with its style ever since de Gaulle, thus entered a less grandiloquent phase that caused some discomfort to some observers. The diplomacy of surprises that had led to meetings with Colonel Khadafi in 1984 and General Jaruzelski in 1985 disappeared.

Yet, political competition remained. The intermittent positioning for advantage in the defense field hurt France's credibility, which Chirac's endorsement of the status quo sought to avoid in the first place. It was often unclear whether statements indicated a change of policy, or were used simply to score points in the struggle for influence over defense or in the quest for bureaucratic support. This situation stifled debate and long-term reflection for the sake of short-term political benefits.[39]

The second hypothesis suggested that the content of the policy will tend to reflect domestic priorities to a higher degree than before. One indeed could suppose (1) that new governing teams will represent new interests, and (2) that both centers of authority will tend to outbid each other for the support of key groups. Because the Socialists rallied to the support of the French arms export industry after 1981, little changed. The Socialists had also strongly defended farmers' interests—despite the agreement to enlarge the Community—and courted a military they largely distrusted. In opposition, Chirac condemned the derailment of the 1984-1988 Military Planning Law and the neglect of conventional capabilities. Yet, although the military budget increased, the 1987 Military Planning Law did not significantly alter this balance. On the contrary, it threatened to cut operating expenditures even further. One year into it, there were already strong indications that its ambitious program would not be fulfilled.

The electoral competition obviously favored powerful and institutionalized groups that parties will hesitate to oppose. It was not that France's foreign policy reflected domestic interests more broadly; rather, the government and the president were less likely to confront them. Electoral competition thus favored the status quo. What was evident in the domestic realm (university reform, prisons, nationality law) applied to foreign affairs as well. Reform of the CAP was more unlikely since it entailed hurting French farmers.

Did parties play a larger role in shaping foreign policy? The UDF was able to pressure the Gaullists and their leader into paying more attention to European questions, although their success was so limited that they have repeatedly warned the government about not implementing its commitments. Rather than a coalition government enhancing the power of the parties, the conjunction of the UDF and president's positions may explain this relative influence. The UDF's positions on defense matters do not seem to have significantly prevailed over Chirac's and Mitterrand's opposition.

Mitterrand's positions did not reflect more accurately the conceptions of the Socialist party. His 1981-1986 foreign policy already included several traditional orientations of the *Parti socialiste*. He also took unexpected stands, and progressively abandoned earlier ones, leaving the party rather confused. Thus, the positions that Mitterrand advanced during cohabitation either did not reflect his party's perspective at all, or at least did not do so more extensively than before. In the end, the party adapted to the president, not the reverse.

The RPR itself was divided. Old Gaullists (Debré, Messmer, Peyrefitte, Foyer) adamantly opposed the "Single European Act." Others argued it would not be implemented. For still others, suspicions about Germany and the desire to preserve the CAP overrode their lack of European enthusiasm. The RPR has traditionally been against the Pluton battlefield missile program, but did not seek to suppress the Hadès, its successor. Many other defense issues—such as the nature of a security guarantee for Germany—were debated within the party. Finally, Chirac did not hesitate to side with the president against prominent members of the RPR or leaders of the UDF (against the April 1986 U.S. raid on Libya for example).

This is not to say that the majority parties played no role whatsoever in the formulation of Chirac's opinions. But the influence of the parties did not seem significantly greater than under a "unitary" regime (that is, an undivided executive supported by a clear legislative majority), in part because doctrinal and policy preferences cut across party lines. Hassner has described the absence of a coherent, well-articulated and purposive right-wing foreign policy characterized instead by "disparate and divergent elements without . . . creative synthesis."[40] The "embattled nationalism" of Michel Debré, the "calm globalism" of Giscard d'Estaing, and the "Reaganesque manicheism" of the younger generation define problems and solutions differently.

The third hypothesis (H3) stipulated that the foreign policy of cohabitation would be less independent. Evidence of lesser independence would mean support for European integration, and a greater willingness to collaborate with NATO allies. Both would conform to UDF preferences and the latter to Chirac's, although many Gaullists would oppose him as firmly as they did Mitterrand.

Was there a trend toward enhanced cooperation with NATO? Certainly, the interests of France and of the United States converged briefly in the early 1980s. Evan Galbraith, the former U.S. ambassador to France, called France America's "best ally" in 1982 and wrote in his memoirs that "Franco-American relations have probably never been better since 1918."[41] The supreme NATO commander praised the Rapid Action Force and the Eureka project on the eve of the 1986 legislative elections.[42] The creation of a Franco-German brigade, the proposed common defense council, and joint maneuvers logically followed the reactivation of the 1963 Elysée treaty which, to some, portended a trend toward closer integration of French defense into NATO's strategy. When the Soviet Union proposed new talks on conventional weapons in April 1986, procedural disagreements between the United States and France prevented the West from responding. Following Reykjavik, however, France showed greater interest in being involved in talks concerning conventional arms reductions. A compromise was reached in June 1987.[43]

The RPR-UDF electoral platform endorsed SDI and urged French cooperation in the program. In office, however, Chirac became more circumspect, encouraging French industrialists' private participation—which Mitterrand had allowed early on—but refraining from signing an official agreement with the Pentagon.

In other areas, France raised fewer issues of contention with its partners. It returned to a position more in line with the rest of the European countries on Central America, collaborated "objectively" with the United States and the United Kingdom in the Persian Gulf, toned down its rhetoric against South Africa, withdrew its objections to the inclusion of terrorism on the agenda of the 1986 Tokyo summit, and signed the Luxembourg convention on terrorism.

France has indeed shown greater reluctance to be isolated. French defense policy has willy-nilly become more interdependent. It could not ignore the implications of the superpowers' behavior and agreements. France's limited resources forced it to take into account its alliance membership and American decisions before making its own choices. Facing a potential denuclearization of Europe, it must build a common front with the United Kingdom and spare the sensibilities of its European partners, especially that of the Federal Republic. Chirac's West European Union initiative of December 1986 amplified earlier efforts by the previous Socialist ministers for external relations. The idea of a European defense was largely accepted by virtually the whole political class, but with wide differences in its definition or in the strategies to achieve it.

Yet, on two occasions, the French government refused requests for tangible support. In April 1986, it rejected the U.S. request for overflight rights to attack Libya (a joint decision by Chirac and Mitterrand which Giscard criticized), but vetoed a UN resolution condemning the U.S. action; and the following November, it refused to break off or suspend relations wih Syria after the United Kingdom had implicated Syria in terrorist activities on its territory.[44]

Regarding European cooperation, France did not press for confrontation and supported conciliatory stands in the trade disputes between the Community and the United States, despite some initial manifestations of resolve. The agreement guaranteeing Americans the retention of their market shares following Spanish and Portugese membership was approved unanimously in July 1986, although France stood to lose by the arrangement. Other trade issues were raised later, but did not prevent a European accord.

It is therefore difficult to ascertain whether independent behavior would have been more pronounced had the regime been unitary. Cooperation was extensive between 1981 and 1986—despite a few *coups d'éclat*—and followed a trend that President Giscard d'Estaing had initiated. The period of cohabitation was therefore unremarkable in that regard.

The fourth hypothesis (H4) suggested that bureaucratic factors would play a greater role in determining foreign policy decisions. Indeed, the Quai d'Orsay hoped to revive a much diminished influence during that period. Its traditional inclination had been to marginalize the prime minister. In recent years, however, it has acted as an intermediary between the Elysée and Matignon, with a tendency to play them against each other in order to free itself from too close a tutelage by either of them.[45] Competition between Mitterrand and Chirac would, they hoped, enhance their informational and supportive role. At the very least, in case of stalemate, the bureaucracy could be called upon to solve the most pressing problems.[46] It was not.

The Quai d'Orsay took a few initiatives that revealed its renewed sense of self-importance. Yet, its role remained limited.[47] A relatively large personal foreign policy staff set up at Matignon to oversee the Ministry of Foreign Affairs and provide independent expertise and information, was often used for sensitive missions such as conducting a dialogue with the United States on defense issues.[48] Moreover, instead of being concentrated within the ministry, foreign policy has become more parceled out. Directly under the prime minister were placed several traditional responsibilities of the Quai d'Orsay: human rights, the South Pacific, parts of cultural diplomacy, and European affairs. The Ministry of Cooperation (foreign aid) also regained its independence from Foreign Affairs, while the international role of the technical ministries continued to grow.[49]

This dislocated foreign policy apparatus promoted bureaucratic conflicts. Turf battles raged. Some agencies sought to force the government's hand, as demonstrated during the diplomatic confrontation with Iran in 1987. Yet, many compromises were reached. The budget of the Military Planning Law, for example, was, as usual, the result of a compromise between the ministries of Finance and Defense.

Competition with the president, lack of time and expertise, electoral priorities, and traditional bureaucratic preferences suggest a certain relevance of the bureaucratic politics model with regard to the advice that Chirac received and accepted. Yet, the president has given himself a preeminent role in defense and European affairs. Support for this hypothesis therefore requires evidence that foreign policy outputs resulted from compromises between the bureaucracies of the Elysée and Matignon. This evidence is limited.

Several factors weaken the applicability of the bureaucratic politics model. To be sure, consultations took place regularly between the two seats of power (Chirac chose his staff to facilitate it), and Mitterrand and Chirac frequently consulted before stating France's official position. Consultation and even compromises, however, are not evidence of the applicability of the bureaucratic model. First, the president's foreign policy staff was even smaller than the prime minister's. Second, the minister for Foreign Affairs reported to the prime minister, not to the president. Third, not only had the influence of the president's advisers been exaggerated in the past, but the personal contacts that his technical advisers enjoyed with their counterparts in other agencies dried up.[50] Their opinion was no longer solicited. They could attend interagency meetings on defense or foreign affairs, but apparently rarely did so.[51] Fourth, Mitterrand was anything but a passive actor in foreign policy.

Bureaucratic conflicts have been endemic to the Fifth Republic, just as they were to its predecessors. The Socialist regime of 1981-1986 was beset by them.[52] Whether they have been more pronounced under cohabitation is still unclear and may vary with different issue areas (how to deal with Iran, for example, produced sharp conflicts among the Interior Ministry, the Quai d'Orsay, Matignon, and the Elysée). Certainly, applying the bureaucratic model as a proactive model of decisionmaking will prove unfruitful. Although multiple advocacy may have increased during cohabitation, significant cultural constraints (socialization, education) still promote conformism. More passively however, the existence of a bureaucratic consensus in certain foreign policy areas (e.g., international economic issues) which in the defense field takes the form of a status quo over weapons programs also worked to limit conflicts and will have a similar dampening effect on future governments or public debate of defense options.

The record of cohabitation on defense and European affairs does not suggest a significant lack of consistency (H5). What was precisely remarkable between the 1986-1987 period was the degree of continuity in relation to earlier policies, as well as consistency in the definition and presentation of French policy, most evident in the security area. Indeed, Chirac took pains to show that the Socialists had rallied to the Gaullian credo or had continued policies defined under the preceding presidency. Even after the sharper regime change of 1958 (an example actually used by the Salmores), de Gaulle did not overturn the basic policy choices of the Fourth Republic until 1965.[53]

Along with a change of style (H1), the hypothesis that is most strongly supported is inertia (H6). This is no surprise, and such a possibility was widely raised before the 1986 elections. It was feared that a traditional conflictual political culture, divergent philosophies, and clashing political interests would create an inevitable institutional stalemate, with disastrous consequences for French foreign policy. Yet, not stalemate, but inertia prevailed. At a time of profound changes in France's environment, the lack of decisiveness was patent. European construction languished. While trade wars with the United States loomed larger, France was unable to take the lead in articulating and defending European interests. Reykjavik did not elicit a more proactive behavior. France largely waited for its partners to react and allowed Margaret Thatcher to acquire prominence in the East-West dialogue, an old French ambition. Few steps were undertaken to solve the defense dilemmas. Far from resulting from clear reflection of the country's needs and priorities, continuity hid an inability to mobilize the country behind specific policies through which France could retain its status as a major power.

Although the prime minister had greater powers, the effective dyarchy instituted by the constitution compounded the tendency of a fragmented regime to lead to inertia. Each party shared power and feared the consequences of conflict. A fragmented bureaucracy tended to pursue traditional policies (as evidenced by the Persian Gulf conflict). Each feared that adversaries would take advantage of any disunity. In the end, agreements hid default positions.[54]

To be sure, decisiveness had not been the hallmark of the Mitterrand presidency, and its vision of the future was often muddled.[55] But cohabitation did not produce a "vision" of what France should strive for and how to get there, at a time of acute international turbulence. The two leaders seemed, at times, to talk past each other. Mitterrand did not actively promote or evoke the European security charter, Chirac ignored Mitterrand's European appeals. Thanks to staff communication and solidarity at various summits (there was a concern for preventing manipulation by third parties), open conflicts and contradictions were avoided. But joint initiatives were also inexistent, each leader leaving the other responsible for his pronouncements and for the promotion of his initiatives. This suggests that rather than multiple advocacy or compromises on fundamental issues, cohabitation created a regime of false pretenses.

Disagreements within the conservative coalition and confusion within the Socialist party, worked to reduce conflicts between the president and the prime minister. It is precisely this diversity of positions on which rest hypotheses about the greater role of domestic groups and the higher dependence of the policy. This diversity appears to have favored inertia in this case. The best way for each leader to maintain some cohesiveness and sense of direction within their own ranks was to continue past policies. Whereas in a unitary regime, internal dissent rarely prevented their predecessors from acting unilaterally and forcefully, the diplomatic and electoral consequences might be so dramatic in periods of cohabitation as effectively to preclude such a possibility.

Cohabitation has shattered many myths about French political culture, policymaking, and the virtues of presidential dominance, and created others regarding consensus. Thanks to the nature of the regime, French foreign policy had since de Gaulle largely been the policy of its leader. A change of institutions created two prisoners of their more powerful predecessors.

Alternative Explanations

What factors, besides regime change, may explain this inertia and mixed support for other hypotheses, and influence the course of policy? One element that may hide the existence of sharp differences in the outputs generated by the two regimes is the short time span considered. For example, even de Gaulle's foreign policy seemed at first in continuity with the Fourth Republic's, and did not cause major controversies until 1962. Furthermore, cohabitation was expected to end in 1988, or even earlier. This prospect increased a reluctance to cause major clashes for fear of an electoral backlash or of undermining the authority of the presidential institution.

Another and much discussed factor is consensus. In 1985, Roland Dumas and Paul Quilès, Mitterrand's last Foreign and Defense ministers, in effect argued that since a consensus existed on defense and foreign affairs, major changes after a conservative victory would be illegitimate, a notion that the opposition of the day naturally rejected.[56] Yet, according to Chirac, cohabitation in foreign policy has been smooth and effective because a consensus exists.[57] If so, one would expect that governments, cohabitationist or not, would display initiative and help mobilize energies behind a certain set of policies. Nothing of that sort happened, however.

This consensus would encompass three distinct spheres.[58] The first one would be a Gaullist consensus illustrated by Mitterrand's and the Socialist party's embrace of the institutions of the Fifth Republic, nuclear deterrence as the solution to French security, opposition to rejoining NATO, and some sort of united Europe. The second sphere would consist of a growing awareness and acceptance of external constraints. This recognition was dramatically symbolized by the 1983 decision not to leave the European Monetary System, the launching of the Eureka program, and the realization that France could not assume her global role without support (in Chad, Lebanon, and in the Persian Gulf). Finally, a more recent aspect of this consensus concerned the totalitarian nature of the Soviet Union and the fear of a German neutralist drift.

But if there is agreement on the vague and unassailable principles of independence, fidelity to alliances, and nuclear-based deterrence, there is little agreement over methods to define and operationalize them, as described earlier. The 1987–1991 Military Planning Law did not solve disagreements over the role of battlefield nuclear weapons, the nature of the French contribution to German security, or the meaning of a European defense. Although there is agreement on the nature of the threat and on the need for nuclear weapons, no consensus has been forged behind a clear strategic doctrine or a set of detailed responses to a changing strategic and economic environment.

The debate over the Planning Law clearly showed the importance of the notion of consensus in the public positions of the French government. The absence of controversies that affected France's neighbors was considered a great strength, but one that had a fragile base (an absence of public debate, relatively low military budgets), which external developments could easily shatter. Its suspected fragility provided a strong incentive to maintain old policy directions in times of great strategic uncertainty and economic constraints. Mitterrand's and Chirac's positions cannot be understood without taking into account the perceived importance of preserving this consensus at home and building one abroad that would justify the French deterrent and prevent the denuclearization of Europe. Thus, it is not the *strength* of the consensus that could explain inertia and continuity, but its *fragility*. [59]

Beyond this, the value of consensus as an explanatory variable seems dubious. Above all, its meaning is unclear. Whose consensus should one examine, the political elite's or the public's? Over what range of concerns? Does it refer to a "broad agreement on some basic principles that define the nation's proper orientation toward the world," or to full agreement on specific actions (Roland Dumas's interpretation)?[60] The broad definition appears more meaningful but may be of little actual value because it can evince different types of explanations and behavior. For example, it can reflect systemic variables (the location of the country, the distribution of power in the system), historical variables (e.g., the Gaullist precedents), or domestic and cultural factors. Further, agreement on tactics does not necessarily imply agreement on objectives. Atlanticists, Gaullists, and Europeanists all favor closer ties with Germany: the first to prepare the de facto reintegration of France into NATO, the second to enhance France's rank, the third to develop an autonomous European pillar. Although all seek to enhance Franco-German cooperation, they do it for different reasons (and support different forms) so that one can hardly speak of consensus.

Mixed support for these hypotheses may also originate in the incompleteness of the regime perspective. How regime characteristics interact with systemic and individual variables matters. Without the institutions of the Fifth Republic, de Gaulle could hardly have undertaken his controversial policies. Yet, it took de Gaulle to use them to their potential. Thus, the qualities identified with presidential regimes may have extrapolated as much from the individual's characteristics as from the regime's. A change of regime will not automatically entail a change of policy. There is little evidence that the nature of the regime *prevented* either Chirac or Mitterrand from initiating changes; but systemic factors restricted their latitude.

Indeed, external variables must figure prominently in any explanation of these findings. The literature on French foreign policy traditionally construes them as constraints that limit policy options. A more extreme position would approach them as determinants of goals and outcomes. The national interest has largely been defined by external factors since 1958.[61] The diffusion of power in the system, European decline, military and resource disparities, the globalization of the international economy, as well as specific policies (de Gaulle's opening up of the French economy), have made France more sensitive and vulnerable to external constraints.[62] For example, although the determinants of arms sales may have evolved from diplomatico-strategic considerations to economic ones, they remained systemic.[63]

A unitary regime was partially able to cope with increased international interdependence by strengthening the state. Yet, Mitterrand had to reverse certain policy initiatives and see major domestic reforms fall under the reality of external constraints. He finally opted to remain in the European Monetary System in 1983. Rather than affecting his predecessor's detachment, he championed the INF cause, cultivated relations with the United States, and took his balance of power perspective to the Bundestag in 1983. The same concern for European solidarity led Jacques Chirac to tone down his criticisms of the 1987 INF treaty. As Lieber concluded, "The example of France indicates that it remains extremely difficult . . . to pursue individual policies which vary significantly from the direction being followed by [her] partners."[64]

Paradoxically, the erosion of U.S. power makes France more susceptible to external constraints. To achieve greater European cooperation on European and defense matters, to fend off U.S. protectionism, to define and pursue security interests that may contradict U.S. ones will require greater sensitivity and adaptation to her partners' concerns. Under cohabitation, Chirac and Mitterrand shared the fear for the future of the French deterrent, the need to preserve U.S. commitment, and concern about potential U.S. withdrawal and German neutralism. A regime of cohabitation is even less capable of controlling the various domestic crosscurrents generated by increasing interdependence; inertia and loss of leadership follow. Progress will result more from the adoption of foreign initiatives (that is, depend on the resolution of internal foreign debates) than from determined and imaginative leadership, or, more likely, it will remain largely symbolic.

A systemic perspective has limits, however. Even if there is consensus on which external forces confront them, decisionmakers always face options. For example, there are different ways of coping with the German "problem." One can build even closer relations with the Federal Republic and support it politically as Mitterrand has done; one can cultivate the relationship with the USSR in the Gaullist tradition; or yet, one can enhance relations with NATO. Significant elements of the French right, along with Prime Minister Thatcher, believe that the best way to counter a German neutralist drift lies not in reassuring the Germans and thus encouraging pacifist movements calling for denuclearization, but in reaffirming the need for those weapons and expressing it through a strong symbolic call for the modernization of short-range nuclear weapons and a doctrine that integrates them into a conventional battle. On the other hand, Mitterrand wants to counter this potential threat through reassurances. This concern explained support for the deployment of Pershing IIs and cruise missiles in 1983, the close dialogue with the Federal Republic (encouraged by the negative British attitude toward enhanced Franco-British cooperation on joint weapon production, nuclear targeting, and submarine patrolling), his more positive response to the INF treaty as opposed to Jacques Chirac's and André Giraud's, as well as his opposition to the debate over the modernization of theater nuclear weapons.[65] Strong systemic constraints exist, but individuals do differ in their appreciation and selection of alternative courses of action.

Conclusion

The examination of these six hypotheses suggests that regime-based explanations have only a limited value in the French context. Four of the six hypotheses are either unsupported by the evidence or the record is unclear. Some of these results stem from the Salmores' assumptions about the characteristics of foreign policy in a unitary regime. For example, policy continuity results as much from the existence of a diversity of actors in the decisionmaking process as from the continuous control of policy by one individual or group. The moderating role of the United States Congress is a good case in point. Moreover, continuity has not been the hallmark of the Fifth Republic, especially under de Gaulle who often changed policy spectacularly. There were dramatic reversals of France's relations with China, Israel, or Great Britain under his leadership. Presidential dominance can also engender incoherence when half-baked initiatives are imposed on the bureaucracy with little follow-up.[66] Unitary regimes may also be closely attuned to the domestic implications of their policies. De Gaulle's policies have been interpreted as rooted in his belief in the need to surmount internal divisions.[67]

The assumption that leaders' policies will be governed by the need to maintain support needs further examination. The records of Mitterrand and his predecessors—all imbued with the ethics of responsibility—indicate that other considerations may often be more influential. There was a widely shared belief before the 1986 elections that the 1988 presidential elections would come to dominate the foreign policy of cohabitation. Predictions originating in this perspective mostly pertained to the process of the policy and were rather unhelpful since electoral considerations could lead one to expect either a very rocky relationship or a smooth one, depending on each protagonist's analysis of the potential payoffs of a confrontation.

Thus, in testing this approach it is difficult to control for other variables. One needs a longer time frame, precise and careful definitions and operationalization of variables, and more cases.[68]

The record of cohabitation suggests that regimes cannot be considered in isolation from individual and systemic variables that may either compound or minimize the effect of institutional changes. To argue that regimes enable change to take place is different from saying that when regimes change, policies will differ. With the reelection of President Mitterrand, the determinants of French foreign policy will be found in the interactions of these three levels of analysis as they have operated since 1986. The president's hold on foreign and defense policies will be strengthened, which will be valuable in dealing with possible changes in U.S. security policy after January 1989. But the conditions under which the security debate will take place have also changed. Cohabitation has strengthened the decline of ideology, leading to a pragmatism that often puts the blame on other governments and emphasizes the short term. The domestic structure has changed since 1981 with a widening of participation, the demystification of the state, and the declining importance of the mediating function of parties. These factors will impede efforts to mobilize support behind more far-sighted policies and hard defense choices even should a Socialist or conservative coalition regain control of the National Assembly.[69] These difficulties will be accentuated if some sort of new cohabitation follows the June 1988 elections and foreign and defense issues are seized upon to bid for centrist voters.

Notes

1. Edward A. Kolodziej, *French International Policy under de Gaulle and Pompidou: The Politics of Grandeur* (Ithaca, N.Y.: Cornell University Press, 1974).

2. For example, Samy Cohen, *Less conseillers du Président—De Charles de Gaulle à Valéry Giscard d'Estaing* (Paris: Presses Universitaires de France, 1980); idem, *La monarchie nucléaire* (Paris: Hachette, 1986).

3. Alfred Grosser, *La IVe République et sa politique extérieure*, 2d ed. (Paris: Armand Colin, 1972).

4. Quoted in Didier Maus, ed., *Les grands textes de la pratique institutionnelle de la Ve République* (Paris: La Documentation Française, 1985), p. 85.

5. Michel Debré, quoted in Maus, *Les grands textes*, p. 5; Charles de Gaulle, in Maus, *Les grands textes* p. 16.

6. Maus, *Les grands textes*, p. 16.

7. Claude Cargai, "Le rôle de Matignon dans les relations extérieures," *Revue Politique et Parlementaire*, No. 916-917 (1985), pp. 111-127.

8. Barbara G. Salmore and Stephen A. Salmore, "Political Regimes and Foreign Policy," in Maurice A. East, Stephen A. Salmore, and Charles F. Hermann, eds., *Why Nations Act—Theoretical Perspectives for Comparative Foreign Policy Studies* (Beverly Hills and London: Sage, 1978), pp. 103-122.

9. Salmores, "Political Regimes," pp. 111-112.

10. Cohen, *La monarchie nucléaire*; Samy Cohen and Marie-Claude Smouts, *La politique extérieure de Valéry Giscard d'Estaing* (Paris: Presses de la Fondation Nationale des Sciences Politiques, 1985).

11. For an illustration under Mitterrand, see Jean-Pierre Cot, *A l'épreuve du pouvoir. Le Tiers-Mondisme pour quoi faire?* (Paris: Seuil, 1984).

12. Maurice Szafran, *Chirac ou les passions du pouvoir* (Paris: Julliard, 1986).

13. Salmores, "Political Regimes," p. 103.

14. Salmores, "Political Regimes," p. 120. This proposition lies also at the core of Pierre Birnbaum's examination of the relationship between the nature of the state and foreign policy. See his "The State Pattern as the Determinant of Foreign Policy," *Jerusalem Journal of International Relations* 6, No. 2 (1982), pp. 36-45.

15. Salmores, "Political Regimes," p. 110: " . . . policy is most likely to be stable and unchanging when there is no change in regime, other things being equal."

16. Ibid., p. 120.

17. See for example, Paul Quilès, "Au delà des fausses querelles," *Le Monde*, 7 March 1986, pp. 1, 23; Maurice Duverger, "Une épée de Damoclès," *Le Monde*, 15 March 1986, p. 2; Pierre Caubel, "La crédibilité du futur décideur," *Le Monde*, 21 January 1986, p. 2.

18. *Le Monde*, 27 March 1986.

19. For example, Cot, A l'épreuve du pouvoir. Régis Debray tried to reconcile these two aspects in *La puissance et les rêves* (Paris: Gallimard, 1984).

20. *Le Monde*, 6 November 1986, p. 28.

21. *Le Monde*, 28 February 1986, pp. 1, 9.

22. Six months after the beginning of cohabitation, Mitterrand reaffirmed his belief that "deterrence strategy is in operation as soon as pre-strategic forces are used." (*Le Monde*, 15 October 1986, p. 8).

23. See Marcel Merle, "La crise de Suez (1956)," in Leo Hamon, ed., *L'élaboration de la politique étrangère* (Paris: Presses Universitaires de France, 1969), pp. 239-252; Alfred Grosser, *Les Occidentaux* (Paris: Fayard, 1978).

24. *Le Monde*, 15 October 1986, p. 3.

25. *Le Monde*, 17 October 1986, p. 4.

26. Mitterrand made this point even as late as March 1987, see *Le Monde*, 1 March 1987, pp. 1, 4.

27. The "charter of the security principles of Western Europe" included five principles:

1. Nuclear deterrence remains the only means of effectively preventing any war in Europe [that is, it must deter both a conventional and a nuclear war].

2. The threat on Europe must be approached globally: nuclear weapons of all ranges, imbalances in conventional and chemical forces.

3. Maintenance of national defenses at a level proportional to the threat is a necessity. The French and British nuclear contributions are essential.

4. Deterrence in Europe rests on the strategic coupling of both sides of the Atlantic as materialized by the U.S. presence in Europe.

5. Disarmament must reinforce security at lower levels of armament through realistic and verifiable agreements. An amended version of the charter that nevertheless responded to French concerns was finally adopted on 27 October 1987 by the Foreign Affairs and Defense ministers of the Western European Union.

28. Pierre Lellouche has aptly summarized the dangers of such a proposition in "La France et l'option zéro: reflexions sur la position française," *Politique Etrangère*, No. 1 (1987), pp. 161–166.

29. *Le Monde*, 6 March 1987, p. 6.

30. *Le Monde*, 11 March 1987, pp. 1, 4.

31. *Journal Officiel*, 9 April 1987, No. 3 [1] A.N. (C.R.), p. 88.

32. Françoise de la Serre, "La politique européenne de la France: new look or new deal," *Politique Etrangère*, No. 1 (1982), pp. 125–138.

33. It should be noted, however, that the 1965 Elysée treaty stipulates that the relations are to take place between the chancellor and the president.

34. *Journal Officiel*, 21 November 1986. No. 109 [1] A.N.(C.R.), p. 6611.

35. Ibid., p. 6623.

36. *Le Nouvel Observateur*, 16 May 1986, p. 20.

37. *Le Monde*, 25 March 1987.

38. *Le Monde*, 14 March 1987, p. 1.

39. This early observation by Thierry Pfister remained largely valid throughout the period of cohabitation (Thierry Pfister, *Dans les coulisses du pouvoir. La comédie de la cohabitation*, Paris: Albin Michel, 1986).

40. Pierre Hassner, "Does the French Right Have a Foreign Policy?" *Telos*, No. 67 (1986), pp. 57–66.

41. Evan Galbraith, *Ambassadeur de choc* (Paris: Stock, 1986), p. 161.

42. *Le Monde*, 23-24 February 1986, p. 7.

43. *New York Times*, 12 June 1987, p. A3

44. In an interview to the *Washington Times* shortly thereafter (published 7 November 1986), Chirac suggested that doubts remained about Syrian responsibility, and claimed that Chancellor Kohl suspected Israeli involvement in the planned bombing of the El Al jet. This was the third time in nine months that the unexpected disclosure of intemperate foreign policy remarks caused him significant embarrassment.

45. Cargai, "Le rôle de Matignon."

46. Cohen, *La monarchie nucléaire*, p. 249.

47. In fact, it may have diminished. Jean-Bernard Raimond did not participate as principal actor in those summits which *both* the president and the prime minister attended.

48. As prime minister under Giscard d'Estaing in 1974, Jacques Chirac had only two foreign affairs advisers, including one for foreign aid, when the minister for Foreign Affairs reported directly to the president in the Gaullist tradition. Yet, whereas Raimond reports to him and shares his criticisms of Mitterrand's past policies, he set up an office of seven advisers in 1986.

49. Measured in financial terms, the Ministry of Foreign Affairs accounted in 1988 for a little less than 20 percent of French external activities (slightly smaller than in 1987). See Jean-François Deniau, *Journal Officiel*, 6 November 1987, No. 78 [1] A.N. (C.R.), p. 5442.

50. See Cohen, *Les conseillers du Président*, ch. 6.

51. Jacques Fournier, "Politique gouvernementale: les trois leviers du Président," *Pouvoirs*, No. 41 (1987), pp. 63–74.

52. Cot, *A l'épreuve du pouvoir*; Debray, *La puissance et les rêves*; Michel Jobert, *Par trente-six chemins* (Paris: Albin Michel, 1984).

53. See Alfred Grosser, *La politique extérieure de la Ve République* (Paris: Seuil, 1965).

54. For example, Samy Cohen argued along these lines at a meeting on cohabitation organized by the Association Française des Sciences Politiques, 3–4 April 1987 (*Le Monde*, 12-13 April 1987, p. 5).

55. Jobert, *Par trente-six chemins*.

56. Quilès, "Au delà des fausses querelles;" Roland Dumas, "La logique

du consensus," *Le Monde, 25 July 1985, p. 1.*

57. *Le Monde,* 8 July 1987, pp. 1, 6.

58. Hassner, "Does the French Right Have a Foreign Policy?," p. 58.

59. Along similar lines, Philip Cerny for de Gaulle and Wayne Northcutt for Mitterrand have argued that the need to maintain a political consensus while key domestic reforms were being implemented was a crucial factor influencing French foreign policy. See Philip G. Cerny, *The Politics of Grandeur. Ideological Aspects of de Gaulle's Foreign Policy* (Cambridge: Cambridge University Press, 1980) and Wayne Northcutt, "The Domestic Origins of Mitterrand's Foreign Policy, 1981-1985," *Contemporary French Civilization* 10, No. 2 (1986), pp. 233–262.

60. Ole R. Holsti and James N. Rosenau, *American Leadership in World Affairs* (Boston: Allen & Unwin, 1984), p. 218.

61. A rigorous application of this perspective can be found in Nicholas A. Waites, "French Foreign Policy: External Influences on the Quest for Independence," *Review of International Studies* 9, No. 4 (1983), pp. 251–264.

62. See Robert J. Lieber, "France: the Limits of Maneuver," paper presented at the annual meetings of the American Political Science Association, 1984.

63. See Edward A. Kolodziej, "Determinants of French Arms Sales: Security Implications," in *Threats, Weapons and Foreign Policy. Sage International Yearbook of Foreign Policy Studies* (Beverly Hills: Sage, 1980), pp. 137–175.

64. Lieber, "France: the Limits of Maneuver," p. 19.

65. *Le Monde,* Sélection Hebdomadaire, No. 2048, 28 January–3 February 1988, p. 3.

66. Cohen, *La monarchie nucléaire.*

67. Cerny, *The Politics of Grandeur.*

68. Although not as competitive, the 1974–1976 "cohabitation" between a centrist president (Giscard d'Estaing) and a Gaullist prime minister (Chirac) could be instructive.

69. Mansbach and Waterman made these points in their general reflections on the impact of changing domestic structures on the Atlantic alliance (Richard Mansbach and Harvey Waterman, "Political Change and the Atlantic Alliance," paper presented at the annual meetings of the International Studies Association, 27–31 March 1984); and Kolodziej, in Chapter 5 of this book, discusses the nature of these choices and external constraints.

CHAPTER 3

Mitterrand, the Socialists, and French Nuclear Policy

JOHN G. MASON

Cohabitation and the Nuclear Presidency

Justice and politics rarely coincide, but there may be poetic justice in the fact that the care of de Gaulle's testament, the Fifth Republic, has fallen to François Mitterrand, de Gaulle's most dogged rival and once the Republic's bitterest critic. Some have suggested that with Mitterrand's election in 1981 the Republic was no longer its original self—that in its place stood instead the Fifth and 1/2 Republic. This notion gained greater plausibility in 1986 when the anomaly of a Socialist government ruling with a right-wing constitution was followed by an even stranger arrangement called *cohabitation*, where France is ruled by two heads—a chief executive divided between a left-wing president and a right-wing prime minister and government. This fragile balancing act has ended with Mitterrand's decisive victory in the 1988 presidential elections. It remains to be seen, however, if a form of cohabitation may not be resurrected by a party coalition between the Socialists and the center-right in the National Assembly and by the presence of right-wing ministers in the Socialist governments of Mitterrand's second term as president. It is not yet clear whether cohabitation represents a lasting mutation of the Gaullist presidential regime or only an episodic deviation from the strong executive system characteristic of recent French political history.

Despite these apparent changes in regime, the last ten years have been characterized by greater continuity than change, and among those things that have not changed is France's steady pursuit of civilian nuclear energy, and the expansion of her weapon stockpiles.

This in itself is hardly extraordinary—all major powers have done the same, at least insofar as nuclear arms are concerned. The fact, however, that France has done so quietly and without much public outcry is exceptional in the West, especially given the doctrinal and policy changes that have accompanied the modernization of French nuclear forces under the Socialists. Public acceptance of French nuclear weapons policy can perhaps be related to its symbolic value as a totem of national modernization and international prestige in a broader sense. Certainly the institutional and technological requirements of a successful nuclear deterrence policy have played a central part in the basic legitimating myth of the Fifth Republic where the "necessities of the nuclear age" have helped justify the centralization of foreign policy in the hands of the president. This successful marriage of national myth and nuclear firepower is the basis of the French variant of the "nuclear presidency."

Over the past twelve years a strong consensus has developed between the leaders of the four major parties (the *Rassemblement pour la République* (RPR) and the *Union pour la Démocratie Française* (UDF) on the right, and the *Parti Socialiste* (PS) and *Parti Communiste Français* (PCF) on the left) around defense issues, which has held together without interruption until the refusal in April 1987 of Communist deputies to join with the other three parties in voting in favor of the 1987-1991 defense budget program. The effect of this consensus has been to give French policymakers great resources for managing public responses to nuclear policy questions. Indeed, they have an unparalleled record of "preempting" opposition to their policies within the Western bloc. The capacity of the French state to pursue nuclear energy development without major opposition has been especially visible over the past ten years given France's apparent "immunity" from the nuclear debates that have plagued nuclear policymakers in other Western countries.

The following discussion will examine the role played by the leftist parties and intellectual elites in facilitating the "normalization" of nuclear weapons development and defense issues, and in promoting a "European evolution" of the interparty defense consensus during the Mitterrand presidency. Collateral issues concerning the exceptional position of France as an "independent" nuclear weapons state in the postwar European system, and its possible erosion in the near future, will also be addressed. Finally we may ask how well public unanimity on issues of nuclear policy will hold up in the face of new international pressures and the modification of both the mission of French nuclear forces and the rules under which the French presidential regime has operated for the past twenty-five years.

French "nuclear nationalism" has supported two related developments: the emergence of a strong presidential regime, legitimated by direct elections, and a strategic policy based on the *force de frappe*. Together they represent fundamental features of the Gaullist political settlement that have endured across a change in political generations (from the generation of the Resistance to the generation of May 1968), and a shift of ruling parliamentary majorities from right to left in 1981, left to right in 1986, and back again in 1988. Michel Debré has argued that these are related developments because without a strong presidential regime the threat to use nuclear weapons would not be credible. And, as de Gaulle once remarked to John Kennedy, without the effective sovereignty that only nuclear weapons guarantee, the chief executive would lack the authority to command his armies' loyalty, or resist the party leaders in the National Assembly.[1] President Mitterrand restated the basic principles of the nuclear presidency when he revised his earlier (prepresidential) view by remarking that "authority to command nuclear weapons cannot be shared. It cannot be shared given French institutions and simply given the nature of the weapons themselves which forbid it—even in France. Deterrence can only exist on the condition that decisions are taken by a single man, and quickly—otherwise it does not make much sense."[2] Perhaps Mitterrand better captured the full aroma of this French blend of presidential politics and nuclear weapons when he stated on state television some years ago that "the keystone of deterrence strategy in France is the head of state, that is myself. All depends on my determination. All the rest is only inert matter." If so, the credibility of France's national deterrent has depended for the past few years on how well a divided chief executive could present a common face to the outside world, and how well a closed nuclear bureaucracy answered to two masters rather than one.

One common view sees the Fifth Republic as a "nuclear monarchy," crediting the French president with discretionary powers in defense and foreign policy unheard of in other Western systems of government. It remains unclear, however, whether these are only presidential powers, or whether they are shared with the prime minister. Under the current constitution, the president is the commander in chief of the armed forces. He alone can order them in and out of action, and can do so virtually without the consultation of anyone but the chiefs of staff, his personal aides, and the prime minister. More importantly, it has become accepted that the president alone can by decree command the French strategic forces into action.[3] This discretion in decisionmaking along with the right to secrecy that covers these decisions from any legislative or cabinet review, gives the French president the widest latitude of any Western chief executive (and quite possibly of any Eastern party leader as well) in decisions concerning the use of military force. The rub is that the constitution has also invested important responsibilities in the hands of the prime minister, who is the head of the secretariat for national defense, and responsible for coordinating all decisions taken by the different agencies with national security responsibilities. As long as they work together the French president and his prime minister represent a uniquely powerful executive. If they do not, power may well travel downward within the national security bureaucracy.

This fine distinction between a strong presidential regime and a strong executive regime has hitherto been moot because the president as the majority leader has always been in a position to overshadow his prime minister regardless of constitutional niceties. However, once Chirac and Mitterrand held the reins of power together, these political restraints no longer applied as in the past, and the aftermath of the 1986 legislative elections has provided some unseemly examples of jockeying for position between the two before and during important international meetings—the Tokyo summit in 1986 for instance, or Chirac's premature announcement of a proposal for a common Franco-German security council in the fall of 1987. By the end of the period of cohabitation, presidential authority over foreign and defense policy suffered a marked erosion as the president and his advisers were sidelined and the Chirac government took more and more initiative in foreign policy decisions. Although presidential power will recover with the installation of the Rocard government, the lack of a clear Socialist majority in the National Assembly makes the stability of the interparty consensus critical not only to the government's survival but also to the integrity of the "nuclear presidency."

The Basis of the Interparty Defense Consensus

The nuclear consensus between the four major French parties comprises five essential principles, three of which are explicitly stated in the preambles of the *Loi de Programmation Militaire* (Military Planning Law), the four-year military budgetary programs presented to the National Assembly.[4] The other two seem implicit in the implementation of these programs, and broadly understood within the party leaderships. Taken together, these principles define a sort of doctrinal orthodoxy, which was refined in the works of military strategists such as Generals Poirier, Beaufre, and Gallois in the 1960s, and diffused over the years by Gaullists and through the missionary work done among French elites by quasi-military bodies such as the Foundation for National Defense Studies or the Institute for Higher Defense Studies.[5] The orthodox strategic discourse has proved useful politically because it stresses the military value of uncertainty as the psychological keystone of deterrence. The doctrinal privilege given to ambiguity concerning French aims and objectives has created an intellectual edifice with plenty of room for different political families to coexist more or less peaceably.

The first principle is that the preservation of French sovereignty requires that France maintain and constantly modernize a strategic nuclear force adequate to deter direct attacks on her national territory. The condition of adequacy, "minimal deterrence," is determined according to the doctrine of "deterrence of the strong by the weak." This principle means that the strength of French nuclear forces need only be proportional to France's value as a strategic stake in the international system, i.e., French forces are deemed capable of intimidating the potential adversary (the Soviets) if they can inflict casualties on them greater than the number of France's own population (i.e., fifty-five million dead).

The second principle defines the limits of minimal deterrence in terms of the doctrine of *le tout ou rien*. French strategists argue that France is too weak to engage in any prolonged war whether nuclear or conventional, therefore her approach to managing any European crisis threatening her security perimeter is first to deter the enemy by using nuclear threats to maintain the existing condition of non-war, and then confront him with a rapid escalation of the conflict beyond the threshold of general war. French strategy seeks to limit the enemy to an all-or-nothing choice on the grounds that both limited conventional or nuclear war-fighting are too destructive for Europeans to tolerate. French orthodoxy eschews any of the recent American elaborations on flexible response, and seeks to limit the use of France's own conventional forces and battlefield weapons to the role of tripwires that would signal the enemy that he is rapidly approaching the point of no return where further action will trigger nuclear strikes on his cities. Accordingly, minimal deterrence involves a commitment to a "countervalue" policy of deterrence by "punishment" and forswears developing "counterforce" capabilities that could ultimately undermine French security by making France too threatening to ignore. It supposes that modest numbers of nuclear weapons allow medium-sized powers to effectively deter superpowers despite the imbalance in their strategic resources. This is presumed to hold true even under conditions where the nuclear strike forces of the superpowers are supplemented by strategic defenses. In the French view, strategic defenses are sufficient to forestall "counterforce" strikes against hardened military targets, but not adequate to stop determined attacks against soft "countervalue" targets, i.e., the enemy's population centers.

The third element in the consensus is the principle of "strategic ambiguity." This means that France should identify neither the conditions under which she would commit her nuclear forces, nor the adversary against which they would probably be used. French sovereignty and security, it is argued, would be compromised if a French government were ever to allow her treaty obligations to NATO, or her German ally, to automatically engage her forces in case of superpower confrontation. Strategic ambiguity, then, is a necessary precondition for preserving effective national control over the decision to go to war. In other words, ambiguity is a necessary consequence of the belief that "deterrence cannot be shared," that France cannot rely on others for her national survival, nor can others rely on her. In the Gaullist discourse, French strike forces are meant to deter attacks on both her national territory, the *sanctuaire national* (designated by French strategists as the "first circle" of France's defense perimeter), and her "vital interests" beyond her frontier, that is, Germany (the "second circle"). While major attacks of any sort (nuclear, chemical, or conventional) on French territory are supposed to trigger immediate nuclear counterstrikes, the threshold represented by her "vital interests" beyond her national frontiers has been left open and unspecified until recently.

This ambiguity, of course, has permitted different party leaderships to pick the enemy of their choice. For the right, and the majority of the Socialists, that enemy is necessarily the Soviet Union. However, for the Communist party, the extreme left, and some currents of the Socialists and Gaullists, the principal political threat has traditionally come from the United States.[6] The principle of "strategic ambiguity," fortunately, has been sufficiently abstract that it allowed all tendencies to be satisfied and to coexist for years, permitting a common strategic discourse to cover up a major point of dissension between party leaderships or, as in the case of the Socialists, between major currents within the party coalition.[7]

This point of dissension is tied to a difficulty: the tension in French strategic doctrine between the need to reassure France's German and U.S. partners about her basic solidarity with them, and her need to preserve the appearance of independent national control of nuclear weapons. In theory, for deterrence to work, foreign alliances must be contingent—France must be free in a crunch to do what her national interest dictates.[8] In its most extreme expression, the principle of "strategic ambiguity" supports a "nuclear nationalism" that can hardly be distinguished from a doctrine of "armed neutrality" (this is a part of the Gaullist legacy greatly cherished by the PCF and the former CERES wing of the PS). This tension, introduces a new division, this time pitting "Atlanticists" against "Nationalists." This division, of course, provides the Communists with their own version of the nationalist card to play against the "Atlanticists," as they have attempted to do recently by playing on anti-German feeling in their criticism of Mitterrand's foreign policy shifts.

French Exceptionalism and NATO

In the eyes of NATO critics, this means that France has become a "free-rider" within the postwar system—happy to sit behind her German *glacis*, and benefit from the "neighborhood effects" of the U.S. system, while pursuing various high-technology prestige projects and independent diplomatic initiatives inside and outside of Europe.[9]

The NATO complaint, heard during Mitterrand's meeting with Khadafi in 1985 and again in 1986 when France refused overflight rights for American F-111's striking Tripoli, underscores the fact that France is exceptional in that she continues to play a visible role worldwide which the other former great powers in Europe have all but abandoned. To borrow a line from Thierry de Montbrial, France appears like the "last of the Mohicans,"[10] the last European power that even pretends to have strategic interests beyond Europe itself. France alone continues to maintain significant military forces outside of Europe in a string of bases that stretches in a belt from Guyana across West Africa to French Polynesia. She alone supports a scientific-industrial complex capable of competing with the superpowers across the full range of existing military technologies and weapon systems. This is no accident because the maintenance of the capability to project force globally and to compete with the superpowers technologically go hand in hand. Although de Gaulle may have wished to substitute high-technology projects for the colonial empire as a new foundation for France's politics of grandeur, today the "confetti" of empire have become critical bases for France's pursuit of advanced technologies. The French nuclear program would have difficulty in replacing the Polynesian testing grounds, and the French space program needs the equatorial launching facilities in French Guyana. These colonial assets outside Europe represent the "third circle" of the French defense perimeter.

As Dominique Moïsi has observed, "France behaves like a mini-superpower,"[11] but the costs of maintaining a colonial presence are rising. The fact that France's presence in West Africa is larger today than at the time of decolonization indicates that the French play the neocolonial game better than most, but the troubles in New Caledonia may only be a foretaste of what is coming in the South Pacific. France appears like the last European "warfare state" in that she retains strategic national ambitions that coexist with definitions framed in terms of personal well-being or social security rather than being totally effaced by them as seems to be the case in the other Western "welfare states."

The fourth element of the party consensus is the "spoiler principle," which concerns the international environment within which French security policy must operate. The French deterrent works best in a context of a stable balance of forces between the superpowers. France's military and diplomatic leverage comes from being able to play as a "free agent" in the international balance—the French decision to commit, or not to commit, her nuclear forces adds an element of uncertainty to the calculations the superpowers can make concerning one another. In crisis situations, the French argue, this principle adds to the stability of deterrence by adding a second center of decisionmaking, rendering unmanageable any attempt by the superpowers to limit a conflict to the European theater alone. In this sense the French *force de frappe* has been presented by some as a pistol pointed as much at Washington as at Moscow.

Ultimately, it is generally understood that French independence depends not only on her own efforts, but also on the preservation of the global strategic balance. This balance, in turn, reflects the interaction between a technological arms race between the superpowers, or conversely their ability to moderate that race through the arms negotiation process. On the one hand, then, France can and must do nothing to support the negotiating process because her own leverage comes from being left out of the superpowers' official calculus of the balance of forces. On the other hand, the future credibility of her strategic forces depends on their success. Here the "spoiler principle" threatens very much to become a double bind, and a nightmare that the Western acceptance of the double-zero option threatens to make real for French policymakers.

The last element of the consensus concerns the domestic

preconditions needed for nuclear deterrence, that is, the strategic role of the consensus itself. This amounts to a prohibition on French politicians saying anything that questions the technical credibility of French strategic forces, or the president's ability to command it in a crisis. Public criticism along any of these lines is seen as undermining the enemy's belief in one's willingness to use deterrence in a crunch. On the grounds that deterrence is essentially a psychological phenomenon that exists in the mind of the adversary, public discussion of its weaknesses has become something of a taboo. At the same time, mismanagement of foreign affairs by the president, or the prime minister, can be interpreted as upsetting the delicate balance of wills with the adversary, and can trigger calls for the government's resignation. As either the Greenpeace or the Khadafi affairs indicated in 1985, incompetence in foreign affairs can be a serious liability for a government already in domestic difficulty. More importantly, the political health of the French executive has now become identified closely with the credibility and ultimately the survival of the nation itself. This fateful association between the nation and the regime both places limits on criticism and heightens its impact when it does occur.

The French sense of their position and responsibilities as the "world's third nuclear power" occupies an important if not central place in the unspoken accord that has united the parties of the left and right around common national goals.[12] It is reflected in the ease with which all parties from the neo-Gaullist RPR to the Communists, refer to de Gaulle's nationalist legacy to legitimate their various programmatic statements. It is echoed in the common satisfaction expressed by party representatives from all corners in France's record of mastering the complex technologies required for the development of thermonuclear warheads, the construction of missile-firing submarines, or commercial space launch vehicles. This shared nationalism may become all the more important to the extent that party elites remain deeply divided in the face of the industrial and social choices they must confront in order to overcome the economic troubles that have interrupted France's phenomenal postwar growth rate (second only to Japan's through the middle 1970s, and now outpaced by the Italians). Ten years of mounting unemployment, capital disinvestment, and increasing ethnic and racial tensions over Third World immigration have worn down the reserves of political capital the major parties can deploy. What remains as a point of unity around which the political class can rally are the themes of "nuclear nationalism."[13] It remains to be seen whether the defense consensus can actually carry all the expectations that party elites seem ready to place upon it.

Taken together, these principles suggest that this internal party accord, founded on a strategic orthodoxy that dates from the 1960s, is vulnerable to external contingencies. Initiatives or setbacks by allies as well as adversaries have as much potential for upsetting the presuppositions of the domestic consensus as for disturbing the international system to which France belongs. As Patrick Viveret has noted, the French nuclear strike force was most "productive," when the international scene was calm.[14] A stable strategic relationship, not confrontation, between the superpowers provided a context within which France was able to maximize the diplomatic leverage that the possession of nuclear weapons offered.

It seems that the Fifth Republic has been doubly blessed. First, during the 1950s, 1960s, and early 1970s it was the beneficiary of twenty-five years of international economic expansion and currency stability. Second, it was favored by the relative stability and equality of the strategic relationship between the United States and Soviet Union. Neither of these external conditions currently favor the continued cohesion of the domestic consensus. France has experienced a steady deterioration of its position in the world market and the apparent erosion of the U.S. nuclear guarantee to West Germany. Sooner than later, if the current double-zero option should ever give birth to a third, France herself may be subjected to powerful outside pressures on her nuclear policy that could produce internal strains. This danger has undoubtedly prompted moves during the Mitterrand presidency to modify the terms of the consensus by a quiet "revolution from above" so as to preempt a future revolt from below, led either by a Communist defection from the ranks of the established parties, or a "pacifist" challenger from outside. Now, of course, the recent splits in the Communist ranks have managed to produce both of these challenges to the unity of the French political class at one time.

Nuclear Nationalism and the French Left

The fact remains, however, that over the past five years challenges to the consensus have failed to appear, and only appear now with the Communists' decision to break ranks long after the popular mobilization around nuclear issues has already receded elsewhere in Western Europe. France has been the only important U.S. European ally that has not witnessed the rise of a social movement with sufficient influence to challenge the monopoly of security policy specialists over discussion of vital strategic questions. In West Germany and the United Kingdom such movements have won over established party and parliamentary leaderships to their antinuclear agenda, and influenced electoral debate, even if they were too weak to actually determine electoral outcomes. Not so in France. The influence of party leaders over the national political agenda and later the pressures of parliamentary discipline once in power, ensured that grass-roots movements were denied institutional support from unions, churches, and the leftist press. In the commercial and state media in France, the anti-nuclear issue has been treated as a foreign affairs story of concern mainly to the extent that it raised questions about German or U.S. reliability. As for French public opinion, the poll data suggest that issues concerning either nuclear weapons or reactors, remain virtually non-issues despite anxiety concerning Chernobyl and the Super-Phenix breeder-reactor.

This French exceptionalism is due in large part to the role leftist party elites have played in helping to keep nuclear issues off the national agenda. This is worthy of note if only because in 1976 these same elites were united in a common program by their formal opposition to both France's nuclear policy and her presidential institution—*la monarchie nucléaire*. In the late 1970s, both Socialist and Communist leaders accepted a reversal of long-standing positions opposing further development of nuclear weapons—a reversal that has also required a revision of their opposition to the presidential institutions of the Fifth Republic. Since then, the Socialist party has generally come to embrace the most abstract version of the Gaullist orthodoxy of nuclear deterrence with all the enthusiasm of the newly converted, as have the Communists, although for different political motives as their decision to break out of the consensus should suggest.

From "Great Refusal" to "Great Reversal"

The decision of Communist and Socialist leaders to reverse their nuclear positions met with only weak opposition—none to speak of among the Communists outside of a few protests and resignations from the *Mouvement de la Paix*, the front peace organization. Some rank-and-file Socialists exercised determined resistance which continued for several years before it was finally swept away by the national leadership during a special party congress in 1978.[15] The actors present and the positions debated at that time still have a certain interest, because they represent the PS's last major internal debate concerning the nuclear issue before the shadow cast by the Mitterrand presidency began to eclipse the internal life of the party.

Before 1978, the French Socialist party was still publicly committed to the phased liquidation of the French nuclear deterrent. A sharp internal division existed between a nationalist/neutralist wing and the old postwar "Atlanticists" over the future direction of French foreign policy, and the party was still unreconciled to the Gaullist presidential regime. At the Paris convention of 1978, a two-thirds majority of the delegates voted for a leadership motion in favor of maintaining the French force de frappe *en état*, thereby reversing the historical position of the party and bringing effective closure to a defense debate that had been going on for several years.[16] The immediate protagonists were a rank-and-file antinuclear lobby with strong ties to the Rocardian wing of the party, a pronuclear group around Charles Hernu with strong ties to the military and François Mitterrand, and finally the CERES group of Jean-Pierre Chevènement. A common interpretation of the defeat of the antinuclear position is to see it as the result of an internal leadership coalition between Chevènement and Mitterrand against the Rocardians motivated by essentially electoral considerations (and this reflects quite well the self-understanding of some participants).[17] But it also represented the culmination of years of lobbying by the small group of defense specialists around Charles Hernu and says much as well about the difficulties created by the political arguments advanced by the party's antinuclear wing that anticipate in significant respects those of the END (European Nuclear Disarmament) in England and the Greens in Germany.

Hernu's group faced a long, uphill struggle—their initial motion in favor of nuclear weapons had received only 15 percent of the votes at the Suresnes conference in 1972 as opposed to the two-thirds majority received in 1978. Their success in overcoming their minority position was due in large part to their early capture of the special party commission on defense and of study groups associated with it. This commission played a critical role as a think tank and a leadership forum, forming a generation of party defense experts who would later move directly into Hernu's cabinet at the Ministry of Defense after 1981, and back again to take over the party apparatus after the Socialist legislative defeat in 1986.[18] (While Hernu himself was removed as Defense minister in the aftermath of the Greenpeace affair in 1985, the definite eclipse of his influence and that of some of his advisers came only in 1987 with the revelation of the Luchaire arms deal with Iran). In addition, the commission ran the party organization within the armed services, *La Convention pour l'Armée*

Nouvelle, which served as a conduit for tapping political advice and professional expertise from within the armed services and the defense establishment. The commission and its allied groups of officers played an important role in the top-down policy process that brought the party around to a pronuclear position. As one antinuclear opponent noted before the 1977 Congress: "One had the impression that instead of creating a Socialist pressure group within the Army, we ended up by creating a military pressure group within the Party."[19] This impression was also shared on the outside. Senior officers associated with the Foundation for National Defense Studies recall that seminars organized by them for the party leadership with Hernu's cooperation were instrumental in "educating" the Socialist leadership to a proper appreciation of defense issues.[20] Hernu's activities not only deflated Socialist apprehensions about the army—putting to rest the phantom of Allende's Chile—but also reduced military fears about the Socialists—helping to establish the ground for the close collaboration that came to exist later between the military and the members of Hernu's cabinet in the Defense ministry after 1981, and that will no doubt be renewed during Jean-Pierre Chevènement's "watch" at the Defense ministry.

The antinuclear wing went into the struggle in 1977 with some public assets: they had the public commitment of the party leadership to renounce nuclear weapons (a key plank of the common program), the support of a broad section of the Catholic left, and the tacit support of the old "SFIO" grouping which had strong "Atlanticist" leanings.[21] These advantages were quickly eroded by the fact that this wing went largely unrepresented in the party's defense commissions. Without the support of the national leadership they were reduced to appealing to local federations and to guerrilla warfare in the small intellectual reviews. Their position was further weakened by the sudden decision of the PCF to reverse its position in conformity with the wishes of its national secretary, Jean Kanapa, in July 1977. Thus, despite the support of some party personalities, the antinuclear wing was destined to win the debate in local organizations, only to lose the vote at the national party congress.

The antinuclear tendency advanced three main objections to a nuclear defense policy. First, they argued that nuclear deterrence is useless militarily against the kind of pressures that the superpowers might bring against an independent Socialist France, i.e., against the threat of economic intimidation by the United States or political destabilization encouraged by the Soviets. Both of these threats could only be addressed by a defense policy that examined the political problem of mobilizing popular forces in solidarity with the

Socialist program.[22] Second, they argued that the reliance on nuclear weapons encouraged the atmosphere of insecurity that could only reinforce Europe's attachment to the bloc system of the superpowers—frustrating European hopes for eventual autonomy from them. Third, they argued that nuclear defense policy reinforced a system of military secrecy and professionalism that was incompatible with the expansion of democratic planning and closed to the possibility of genuine popular participation in national self-defense. Taken together, nuclear defense was seen as in total contradiction with the project of building a self-managing society. This critique anticipated themes (popular sovereignty, non-nuclear defense, and European "self-determination") that would later be picked up by the antinuclear movement elsewhere in the 1980s. The antinuclear critique was summarized by a declaration in *Alternatives Non-Violentes*, the antinuclear newsletter, which attacked directly the nuclear presidency: "A nuclear society will be fatally centralized and based on secrecy. It will be a society where the preservation of the liberties of the citizen body will be surrendered to the judgement of a few men, and in the last analysis to the decisions of one man alone."[23] The refusal of nuclear weapons was tied to the rejection of France's presidential regime at the very moment when the Socialist party leadership was preparing the election of François Mitterrand to presidential office. The antinuclear wing represented a rejection of the deepest aspirations of the party leadership and was necessarily rejected in turn. It had little place in the presidential party the PS had become. Its future, if it had one, would lie outside the party in an independent social movement, and some of its members would finally find their place in the noncommunist peace organization, CODENE, the French affiliate of the END campaign.

The 1978 "rallying to the bomb" seems like a clear victory for the partisans of the *force de frappe*, but the party motion that carried the day was a compromise document that tried to satisfy as many groupings within the party as possible. First it contained one concession to the antinuclear feelings within the party—it admitted that the concept of deterrence was in crisis and committed the party to a long-term search for a replacement. Second, the motion accepted all the practical policy recommendations of the special party commission headed by Hernu, and committed the future Socialist government to maintaining nuclear forces adequate to defend French independence. Finally the party committed itself to a major reform of the system of military conscription and national service, and to a reorganization of France's conventional forces along the lines of a decentralized system of local territorial militias based on popular mobilization. This plank was a concession to the CERES wing and helped cement the left wing's adherence to the new direction.[24] It was justified in terms of socialist tradition by the reference to the need to broaden the base of national defense through reliance on mass mobilization, a fundamental political principle since the time of Jean Jaurès's *l'armée nouvelle*.[25] This was intended as a gesture to the enduring fears of the party traditionalists concerning the reactionary character and political unreliability of the professional army, *l'armée de la caserne*. The purpose of politicizing the country's territorial defense can always be understood as an avenue for creating a "parallel" military organization to frustrate any plots by "internal enemies." These ideas of territorial defense, of course, did not fit very well with Hernu's attempt to seduce the regular army, nor did they have much place in a nuclear defense program oriented toward the perfection of "forces in being" and dependent on a small cadre of highly skilled professionals.

The party position on defense that emerged from the 1978 congress was a compromise that used the language of the most abstract version of nuclear deterrence doctrine to endorse the *force de frappe*. Following the principle of all or nothing it proposed a cheap path to achieving European security by using French forces to "disarm" the superpowers' presence there. It proposed a theory that reasoned in terms of using French nuclear assets to maintain the condition of non-war and to cancel out the utility of military forces as war-fighting instruments. It sought to insulate France "today" from the effects of the postwar system of alliances, while promising disengagement "tomorrow" for Europe.[26] Taken as a whole, this rationale for nuclear weapons taps the same themes: the fear of war-fighting and the desire for an independent Europe, which have been exploited elsewhere by pacifist movements. It may come as no surprise that *Nous les Grands*, the tract written by Hernu explaining the argument in full, was withdrawn from circulation shortly after the Socialists came to power. However, despite the naivete of some of its claims, this position already hints at the European concerns of later Socialist policy.

More immediately, this compromise is as interesting for what it does not say as for what it does. It passes over the important internal division within the party concerning the Atlantic alliance by avoiding any discussion of the specific strategic choices a socialist government would face in Europe. Relying heavily on the principle of "strategic ambiguity" already mentioned, the party leadership was able to postpone any choice between the "nationalist" (anti-

American) orientation of the CERES, which would maintain France's diplomatic independence through a kind of nonalignment, and the "Atlanticist" (pro-American) SFIO wing of the party, which would seek closer coordination of French forces with France's NATO partners.[27] By accepting a version of the official strategic orthodoxy, the party leadership was able to allow the CERES and the SFIO to have the enemy of their choice. The effect was to make orthodoxy in nuclear strategy the keystone to an internal party compromise central to Mitterrand's coalition within the party, and useful vis-à-vis the Socialists' Communist allies. The fragility of this compromise provided few incentives for debate or original thinking within party ranks. The tendency toward dampening debate was deepened during the Mitterrand presidency by the "hollowing out" of the party's international and defense organs, as the best talent was systematically creamed off by government ministries, and by the atrophy of internal debate at party congresses. The PS increasingly came to represent government positions at home and abroad,[28] just as, at the same time, the ideological themes of third-worldism and nonalignment, which had colored the PS's electoral propaganda, were displaced by a "strategic" discourse more suited to explaining governmental policy.

The possibility of challenges from the outside are also limited by the positions adopted by the Communist party that rallied to the nuclear consensus even before the Socialists had completed their reversal. The Communist approach to the nuclear question was in a sense quite straightforward. They have supported the consensus to the degree that French nuclear forces provide a rationale for the nonintegration in NATO, and a foundation for France's future neutrality in any European crisis. The Communists have argued for the most extreme version of the nationalist neutralist outlook on French policy.

This did not present them with any insurmountable difficulties until the party found itself obliged to argue simultaneously for France's independence from the postwar alliance system, and for the basic justice of the Soviet demand that French nuclear forces be included in the forces to be negotiated, at the Geneva INF talks.[29] Similarly, for most of this decade, the Communists found themselves obliged to restrain the development of the French peace organizations in order to keep their four cabinet seats. This placed them at odds with the leadership of one of their important front organizations, *Le Mouvement de la Paix*, which they have brought to heel by creating a competing organization, *L'Appel des Cents*. The party voted for the Socialists' defense budget (which named the USSR as France's only adversary), and restrained their own peace organizations' participation in demonstrations against French nuclear policy. At the same time, the party encouraged demonstrations against the deployment of U.S. missiles elsewhere in Europe, while a member of a French government that supported such deployment. This double-game was hard to maintain and certainly contributed to the party's eventual break with the Socialists in 1984. The party now feels free to take new positions that will at least have the virtue of being internally consistent, and better positioned to take advantage of the current Soviet initiatives in this area. However, even fascination with Mr. Gorbachev may not be enough to compensate for the erosion of the party's influence, as the miserable score of its candidate in the 1988 presidential elections attests. In view of the disappearance of the Communists as a distinct parliamentary group, the party may become so marginalized that its positions no longer matter.

The fact that both the Socialists and Communists passed into formal opposition in 1986 reduced the pressures on rank-and-file members to conform to government policy, thus restoring a possible space for social movements. But given the "cohabitation" between a Socialist president and a right-wing government, this space has not been very wide, and has been occupied by movements like *SOS Racisme*, closely related with the cultural apparat of the Socialist party.[30] The presidential campaign altered this to the extent that Mitterrand felt inclined to make some concessions to the feelings of left-leaning voters on arms control issues. But the impact of any modulations of the presidential rhetoric did not go beyond endorsing the Soviet-American INF deal, and reaffirming the orthodox French position against the tactical use of nuclear arms as battlefield weapons.[31]

Nuclear Consensus and Intellectual Mutations

Beyond the world of leftist party elites, the French defense consensus has received critical reinforcement from a cultural shift among the intellectual left that has undermined the legitimacy of any "leftist" challenge to the reigning strategic orthodoxy. The attitudes of intellectual elites are an important cultural force in France, creating real constraints in the general climate of opinion within which party leaders must operate. In the 1950s for instance, the official political world was anticommunist and pro-American (Atlanticist), at a time when the intellectual world identified with the "socialist camp," i.e., with its own Communist party and the international communist movement. In the 1970s, in contrast, the official world under Valéry Giscard D'Estaing was still sufficiently Gaullist to be vaguely anti-American and "soft" on the Soviets, at a point when the intellectual world was undergoing a sea-change in its fundamental view of communism and the Soviet Union.

In the early 1980s, this tension continued, only it was focused on the official socialist left which oscillated between a relatively "hard" line on the Soviets in foreign policy, and a soft line vis-à-vis its domestic communist allies. A new intellectual sensibility emerged, that of the "antitotalitarian left," and contributed greatly to the collapse of Marxism as a legitimate political discourse, and its replacement by a liberal discourse in economics and a "republican" discourse in politics. More importantly, it has had a significant impact on the political culture of the Socialist party, helping to remove the ideological barriers that stood between it and certain tendencies of the center-right, and has occupied the social and institutional space that in other European countries has been filled by the peace movement.

The belated discovery of the "Empire" in the neighborhood, and the scandal of French intellectuals' postwar complicity in the defense of the Soviet system in Eastern Europe, have absorbed energies that might otherwise have been enlisted in the French equivalent of the antinuclear campaigns of the early 1980s. The fact that the attention of the French intellectual left was fixed on the drama of the Gdansk shipyards, or the battles around Kabul, when others were looking at the deployment deadlines of cruise and Pershing missiles is not news. But it is worthy of mention if only because it helped erase in elite circles the Gaullist idea that the postwar systems created by the Americans and the Soviets were in some way equivalent, and that the best policy for France was to seek a position of equal distance between them.[32] Indeed, this shift in the intellectual wind, exemplified for instance by the conversion of such left-wing warhorses as Yves Montand into apostles of the Soviet peril, encouraged a hardening of public attitudes toward the Soviet Union and a total reassessment of the global role of the United States. This remains true given the fact that the intellectual public in France has received the Soviet "new look" with a much greater degree of skepticism than seems to be the rule among other Western Europeans.

The diffusion of the antitotalitarian critique of Soviet style "state socialism" within the Rocardian wing of the PS and the Catholic left marked a break with the traditional Marxist culture of the PS that had informed the party's earlier evaluations of the strategic balance and threats to France and colored much of the CERES-inspired *Projet Socialiste* of 1980. The antitotalitarian view of Soviet society stressed the absence of liberal political institutions and norms, and the central place occupied by the military and police apparatus in party/state's system of domination over Russian society. The Soviet Union emerges from this critique as a fragile but ruthless dictatorship standing at the center of a bureaucratic empire that has extended its frontiers into the very heart of Europe.[33] Unable to compete with the liberal democracies on its periphery, this empire is seen as requiring military superiority in Europe to maintain its hold over its European satellites, and to intimidate the independent societies lying beyond its direct control. The chief threat facing France, then, does not come from the United States but from the empire that dominates the central European heartland of Western civilization.[34] The United States is seen as a failing hegemonic power, and its apparent recovery under Reagan a welcome event. The U.S. presence, in any case, must be supported until such time as Western Europe finds the will to undertake its own defense, and to begin the struggle to force a Soviet retreat from Prague, Budapest, and Warsaw.[35]

While it is unlikely that intellectual outrage with the Soviet presence in the heart of central Europe is widely shared in *la France profonde*, over the past ten years one of the anomalous features of French public opinion has quietly disappeared. French public opinion polls no longer show as much distrust of the United States as of the Soviet Union, or significant reserves of good will concerning the Soviets remaining from World War II.[36] Indeed, public perceptions of Soviet hostility have kept pace with the changes in official policy and with those in intellectual circles.

This moral political awakening is still mainly a development limited to the intellectual left in Paris, but it has had important effects nevertheless. It undermined the moral authority of the 1978 Socialist compromise by working to delegitimize the nationalist discourse of "nonalignment" that provided the rationale for the Socialists' simultaneous acceptance of the *force de frappe*, and ambivalence toward the Atlantic alliance. By adding the force of their moral argument against the Eastern bloc to the "neo-Gaullian" discourse already adopted by the party defense experts, they also helped create the articles of reconciliation between the Rocardians, Mitterrandists, and "Atlanticists." At the same time, these developments made the electoral alliance with the Communists increasingly difficult—it kept on stumbling over Kabul and Gdansk. Finally all these trends contributed to the marginalization of the CERES by shifting the intellectual climate against their nationalist/

neutralist discourse, and by eliminating their role as privileged intermediaries with the Communists.

At the same time, the antitotalitarians desanctified the antinuclear position that was identified in their minds with the basest kind of retreat from political values. As Paul Thibaud editorialized in *Esprit*, the review of the Catholic left: "Pacifism involves giving no positive value to peace beyond reducing human life to simple human survival. It cannot be enough to do what we can to see that human life should continue. We must act so that it can also be a humane life, that is, a free one."[37] Pacifism is identified with a willingness to sacrifice all political values on the altar of peace—a peace with the Soviets compromised by the Pacifists' willingness to accept peace on Soviet terms. The slogan of *Esprit*, "the Masquerade of the Dictatorships is finished: Change Culture and Politics," says much about the ability of the antitotalitarians to occupy the moral ground within the Catholic and non-Marxist left that otherwise might have been left open for other movements. The noncommunist antinuclear movement in France saw its best troops in the church and the independent trade unions lost to it the moment they were won over to this moral and political revival of left-wing anticommunism.

More importantly, perhaps, the antitotalitarian left initiated an influential debate about the political meaning of the rise of pacifist movements in Western democracy. This focused the attention of French intellectual elites on the problem of the vitality of the *esprit de défense* underlying the nuclear consensus of Western society. It raised the larger problem of the interrelation between national defense, public opinion, and nuclear weapons, asking whether nuclear deterrence did not ultimately erode the public confidence necessary for maintaining a vigorous national defense effort. This question was asked not only for France but in particular for West Germany, focusing on her future reliability as a security partner for France. The antitotalitarians defended the notion that in the German case the rise of the peace movement was a form of displaced nationalism, and this formulation gave the Mitterrand government a political rationale that went beyond the existing strategic ones to guide its new European orientation to France's foreign policy.[38]

Nuclear Nationalism and French Public Opinion

Recent French studies of public opinion trends in West European countries relate the capacity of the peace movements to mobilize support to two factors: the degree to which a particular national public feels dependent on U.S. protection, and the strength of public awareness about the danger of a superpower confrontation in the near future.[39] French public opinion patterns differ because French respondents were not so concerned by the risk of nuclear war (they are more concerned about U.S. interest rates or the superpowers' rivalries in Third World countries), and because they felt the least need for U.S. protection.[40] Furthermore, very high levels of support for France's nuclear strike forces coexist with the widespread refusal to ever consider its use "even in the case of invasion."[41]

This mix of public attitudes in France has been open to two interpretations: a theory of "responsible nationalism," and a theory of "nuclear pacifism."[42] The "responsible nationalism" interpretation is promoted by spokespersons for the Socialists and the right alike. It views the relative calm of the French public as a sign of its basic good sense, and confirmation of the wisdom of de Gaulle's decision to distance France from NATO by replacing the U.S. nuclear umbrella with something of local manufacture and greater reliability. According to this view, the disorder that one saw elsewhere was the inevitable but wrong-headed reaction of people who had been betrayed by the irresponsible policies pursued by their own governments over the course of a generation. These governments allegedly forfeited their peoples' confidence the moment they gave up national control over basic defense policy in exchange for U.S. protection. This bad exchange not only wounds national pride, but it delivered a lesson in political irresponsibility that came back to haunt them in the form of a "pacifist/defeatist" turn in public opinion the moment the world scene became a little rocky at the beginning of the 1980s. France is free of this "defeatism" because it won her people's trust by pursuing a policy of national responsibility in defense. These analysts point to the high levels of support this policy enjoys in the opinion polls, and to continued public tolerance of high defense budgets and very low levels of draft evasion, as evidence that this consensus is not limited to elite groups. This is viewed only as France's just reward for having defended her national virtue for a generation.

The "nuclear pacifism" school reads the same poll data differently.[43] In this view, it is the Gaullist nuclear orthodoxy which has given rise to public attitudes which, while pro-nuclear, are as escapist as elsewhere, and just as rooted in "magical" thinking. "Magical" thinking here means that the French public has distorted nuclear deterrence to mean that wars are now ruled out, that deterrence is equivalent to a permanent state of "non-war." Further, the ambiguities of French nuclear doctrine permit people to imagine that, if war did come, France has the means to stay out by abandoning her allies and withdrawing into the national nuclear "sanctuary." These analysts argue that the public has quite accurately perceived "nuclear nationalism" as a doctrine of "armed neutrality," which has the added advantage of being nuclear and making any active citizen participation in the defense of the national territory irrelevant. Public support for France's nuclear deterrence turns into its opposite, a "pacifist" fantasy that French citizens will be spared the dirty business of war, at least on their own territory. This school expects public support for France's nuclear forces to erode as soon as real-world events begin to puncture the French public's sense of being immunized against the risks of history. Ironically, the same poll data indicating public support of the draft also provide evidence to support this second interpretation as well—apparently the French approve of national service because they associate it with individual social mobility rather than preparation for actual combat.[44] The existing consensus is condemned because it leaves the French demoralized by a defense doctrine that transfers all real responsibility for national defense to the president of the Republic and a few missile crews. The citizen is seen as stripped of all responsibility, unready to participate in the life of the nation, leaving French policymakers politically disarmed, and unable to confront any real crisis situation.

Both of these interpretations are exaggerated in their common misreading of social movements elsewhere in Europe as movements for "preemptive surrender" to the Soviets, and both assume that there are no meaningful defense alternatives to nuclear weapons. They may, however, suggest what is going on with French public opinion. The nationalists are probably right to underscore the connection between levels of public support for nuclear policy and the distance with which most French view U.S. political leaders and policy debates. French public opinion has not felt involved in U.S. policy disputes about limited nuclear war-fighting that helped drive up levels of public anxiety in the rest of Western Europe. At the same time, this feeling of "distance" supports the idea that the French entertain ideas of a quasi-magical "immunity." The reading of this attitude as a form of "nuclear pacifism" suggests that policy changes that bring France into closer collaboration with U.S. policy could have unpredictable consequences for the public's current peace of mind. Such moves would at least make U.S. policy debates more visible. Closer collaboration could also imply that the international environment has become so dangerous that French leaders consider it prudent to join the collective rush for shelter. Such perceptions might tend to increase the public's awareness of the reality of security threats, again with unpredictable political effects.

In many ways the French mix of public apathy and effective elite control over nuclear policy discussions resembles the situation in virtually all the Western political systems until recently. Public sensitivity in other European states may seem like an extraordinary episode when viewed against the public indifference to nuclear policy during most of the postwar period. There have been waves of public concern in the 1950s and 1980s when the relations between the blocs have been particularly tense. But as the most recent upsurge of antinuclear activism recedes, French exceptionalism seems less atypical than it did when viewed against the backdrop of the Euromissile deployment (the effects of Chernobyl may modify this equation for some European publics).[45] The one abiding difference between the current situation and previous ebbs and flows of public concern is that this one seems to have left permanent traces on party doctrine. In Germany and Great Britain, the antinuclear movements have left their mark on party platforms and party cadres in ways that may long outlive the lifespans of the movements themselves—in much the same way as the French leftist parties were marked by the programmatic themes of May 1968 well into the late 1970s. The French Socialists have recognized this mutation elsewhere in Western Europe and are trying to overcome their isolation by finding common ground with other socialist parties around the themes of European sovereignty.

Mitterrand's Defense Policy:
The End of French Exceptionalism?

France's position among the U.S. European allies is exceptional because she is the only continental European state with nuclear weapons. France is also exceptional in that she came out of World War II, in which she was one of the greatest losers, as one of the few states who won something real from the postwar peace. Finally, France seems privileged because she appears to occupy the position of a "free-rider" in the postwar security arrangements.

France gained much from World War II. The defeat of Germany meant that her greatest geopolitical rival was divided into bits of more manageable size (in the words of one French foreign minister: "We love Germany so much, we want two of them"). It also meant that for the first time since the Napoleonic Wars France's security perimeter fell on someone else's national frontier, West Germany's, rather than her own. Finally, the security cost of Germany has largely fallen on the United States, which has both maintained an important body of troops on the ground and extended a nuclear guarantee.

Under de Gaulle's leadership, France improved on these gains by developing her own national nuclear technology and credible delivery systems to carry them. More importantly, de Gaulle succeeded in withdrawing France from the NATO military command and in negotiating the withdrawal of U.S. troops, equipment, and support facilities from French soil. This makes France virtually the only U.S. ally in Europe with no U.S. troops or weapons stationed on her soil. This means that France has not allowed her security tie to the United States to impair her national control over her choices of defense strategy, the deployment of her national forces, or the development of weapons systems and military technology.

Compared with other European state systems of defense planning, which are so tightly intermeshed with the U.S. system that they sometimes appear as subsystems of their superpower partner, the French system of national defense planning seems remarkably intact. This relative autonomy within the U.S. system has paid off in the form of diplomatic dividends in the Third World and, to a lesser extent, in Europe itself, which in turn reinforces France's technical and military independence by increasing the French penetration of available markets for arms sales. As the world's third largest arms supplier after the United States and the Soviet Union, the French have been able to use sales abroad to support the financial weight of the technological effort required to remain militarily competitive with the superpowers across a broad range of advanced weapons systems. We should note, however, that their ability to keep this up indefinitely has been called into question by the drying up of the Middle East arms market outside of Iran and Iraq and by the entry into the world arms market of other arms producers such as Brazil, China, and Great Britain—all of whom have cut into France's share of the remaining Third World markets.

However, France's deterrent policy is vulnerable to an acceleration of the superpowers' technological competition, which could threaten the technical credibility of the French forces. Hence, France needs certain arms talks to succeed, especially those concerning the deployment of large-scale ABM defenses, or antisatellite weapons. At the same time, France's ability to keep expanding and modernizing her own nuclear forces could be threatened by a successful arms agreement between the superpowers that might lay the foundation for taking the nuclear forces of the other three nuclear powers into account. Changes in the international environment could easily generate pressures directly along the fault lines buried beneath the surface of the domestic consensus, provoking political tremors. Such an eventuality is likely as the size of France's nuclear forces continues to grow. It is anticipated that French firepower will multiply five times over the next five years to some six hundred warheads and possibly a thousand tactical warheads, neutron bombs, and "mini-nukes." As French nuclear capacities diversify allowing for some counterforce capability at the top and increasing battlefield interdiction capabilities at the bottom of the nuclear escalation ladder, so will international visibility and pressures from the international community increase, as both the Greenpeace affair and the history of the INF negotiations already suggest. The evolution of conventional military technologies in directions that might allow France to replace nuclear weapons for certain counterforce and interdiction missions, and the moves toward the "denuclearization" of theater forces in Western Europe may well result in a hostile international climate for the further development of French nuclear forces. The international conjuncture that allowed the French exceptional autonomy for their nuclear policies and immunity from international criticism may well be coming to an end.

Under Mitterrand, French foreign policy has moved increasingly toward a renewed effort to build greater European unity around the pole of Franco-German cooperation. Symbolic in this regard has been his attempt to breathe new life into the Western European Union, the European defense organization that has been largely moribund since the 1950s. At the same time, Mitterrand has given particular emphasis to assuring France's German ally about her understanding and support of Germany's defense needs—a solidarity he has sought to express by deeds such as his Bundestag speech in 1983, and gestures such as the revival of the 1963 Franco-German defense accord signed by Adenauer and de Gaulle. While this policy is aimed primarily at West Germany, it necessarily involves greater cooperation with Germany's principal ally, the United States. The French have learned the futility of forcing Bonn to choose between Paris and Washington, so in order, perhaps, to leave the Germans free to choose both Washington and Paris, bilateral relations between France and the United States have grown in pace with the growth of Franco-German relations.

Mitterrand has also moved France away from the position of "strategic ambiguity" so dear to French strategic orthodoxy. In the 1984 *Loi de Programmation*, the Soviet Union is identified for the first time as France's only major strategic adversary. At the same time, France has increased the visibility of her commitments to German security by publicly declaring for the first time that the defense of Germany's eastern border is a "vital national interest" for France, thereby implying that French nuclear weapons might be used if that border were ever violated.[46] This implicit nuclear commitment has been strengthened by the creation of the Rapid Action Force (FAR) which is composed primarily of helicopter and ground antitank forces designed for rapid insertion in the invasion route across the North German plain. However, the integration of French marine and paratroop units, traditionally reserved for Third World missions within this new force has given French policymakers a fig leaf, allowing them to claim that this force has an overseas expeditionary role, and that it does not necessarily exist only for a German mission.[47] At the same time, French spokesmen have implied that the Second Army Corps with two armored divisions stationed at Baden-Baden is now available to act alone or with the FAR as an armored reserve for NATO forces in Germany, and that together with the First French Army based inside France but close by the border, this armored force represents the second largest conventional contribution to Germany's defense after that represented by the Americans. This willingness to discuss French conventional units as having more of a role than simply opening "a national deterrence maneuver" following the hypothetical collapse of NATO's central front represents a major rhetorical shift, which has been backed up to a limited degree by concrete measures.

The Germans have responded by hosting in September 1987 "Bold Sparrow," the largest Franco-German joint maneuvers in postwar history, in which twenty thousand troops of the FAR entered Bavaria to join German units already engaged in repulsing an hypothetical invasion from Czechoslovakia. The Germans have also proposed the creation of a Franco-German brigade, outside the NATO integrated command, in which German troops would serve under a French commander. This proposal has elicited signs of interest from other parties as well, including even the Spanish whose concerns have traditionally been far removed from the integrity of the German frontline. Lest one think that the brigade is all icing and no cake, the official French response to this proposal has been to accept exploratory discussions on the condition that it would be sheltered under the "umbrella" of French nuclear weapons—a "generous" offer the Germans seem reluctant to embrace. In the meantime, the keepers of the temple of orthodoxy back home in France have denounced these moves toward a form of "enlarged sanctuary" as reckless gestures by leaders whom General Gallois has characterized as having "big hearts and little heads."[48] It is safe to assume that the general speaks for more than himself, and that his reaction is shared not only by some in the military but also by some in the ranks of Chirac's RPR.

In terms of nuclear systems, this policy shift coincides with the production of a new medium-range tactical missile, the Hadès, capable of striking East European targets from inside France's eastern border, and with the completion of research and development of neutron warheads that can be fitted to both the airborne ASMP attack missile and new 55-millimeter artillery shells. New generations of battlefield weapons, including "mini-nukes" as well as neutron warheads, are now ready for production and deployment in the hundreds if not thousands,[49] and indeed their production may have already begun without any official announcement.[50] This strongly suggests that the French risk breaking out of their traditional stand of "minimal deterrence" from the bottom of the escalation ladder if not from the top. The sense of heady new potentialities has been reflected in declarations by certain right-wing representatives who now speak quite easily of *la dissuasion du fort au fort,* and propose the stationing of French conventional units equipped with a full array of tactical nuclear weapons alongside frontline NATO units on Germany's eastern frontier.[51] In any case, the new visibility of France's commitments to German security presses directly along the old fault lines of the interparty consensus and has led the French Communists to withdraw into a position of strategic dissidence (some would say irrelevance)—something France's nuclear weapons programs never caused them to do. It has also encouraged Pierre Juquin to make the nuclear weapons question the centerpiece of his 1988 presidential campaign at the head of a cartel of movements and parties of the extreme left.[52]

The Mitterrand government ran these domestic political risks partly to consolidate Germany as a future security partner (and to keep her as the frontline state standing between France and danger), but also because it was convinced that France could no longer afford to stay in the strategic and technological race using only her own national resources. The size of the SDI research budget alone is equivalent to the total yearly budget for all of France's strategic programs.[53] This difference in the resource base has impressed many French policymakers with the difficulties involved in supporting the growing costs of continued competition in high-technology fields. They are convinced that they cannot do so without German support, but also believe that only France has retained the political "will" to continue the effort to stay in the race as an independent player. This policy is presented to French public opinion as a kind of Gaullism on a European scale—a sentiment expressed in London in 1987 when Mitterrand declared: "France is my fatherland but Europe is my future." Its full meaning may have been better stated by a young French defense analyst who once remarked to me: "France must build Europe in order to save her own skin." So far the idea that these changes represent more than a "slight modification" of French declared policy seems to have passed unnoticed by the French public, although recent polls have shown surprisingly high levels of support for increasing French cooperation with Germany and France's level of commitment to Germany's defense.[54] This new European twist on the old Gaullist doctrine is now reflected in the defense programs of all the major parties except the Communists. It will, however, demand a more sophisticated mix of the themes of European cooperation and the pursuit of independence from the superpowers than the old consensus seems to allow.

Some effort at renewal seems necessary. Already the Reagan SDI program has caught the public's imagination in France like nothing before. This creates a hint of public doubt about the future credibility of France's nuclear deterrent force, and has prompted calls for France to throw in with the U.S. competition before it is too late.[55] Indeed, conflicts between Chirac and Mitterrand over the direction that French policy should have taken concerning collaboration with the U.S. SDI program were among the rare disputes to mar cohabitation in defense and strategic policy.

This suggests that outside realities are beginning to affect the closed world of French deterrent doctrine in ways that are politically significant for the first time in recent memory. This must be a troubling sign, because it implies that the defense agenda has escaped the control of the information managers. Foreign information and ideas are likely to continue to seep in to trouble them further as French collaboration with the Americans and with other Europeans continues to develop. The fact that French elites have recognized this problem was confirmed in the fall of 1986 by a series of calls for a major new effort to counter "foreign disinformation campaigns" aimed presumably at weakening public confidence in the national deterrent force.[56] It seems safe to assume here that French elites are probably as much concerned by antinuclear "disinformation" of U.S. or German origin as by the more familiar effort they have expected from the Soviets.

The French face hard choices with limited resources in the years ahead. Already there are divisions within the concerned bureaucracies about the choice of follow-on strategic systems for the

1990s. Some want to develop a French version of the cruise missile, based on the existing ASMP (medium-range air-to-ground attack missile); others wish to add more missile-launching submarines to France's existing fleet of six; still others want a nuclear-powered aircraft carrier, and others a mobile land-based missile, the SX, similar to the SS 20. The list goes on to include reconnaissance satellites and possible antisatellite weapons. It is not at all clear how much of this France can afford and still garrison her overseas possessions. Development decisions for the systems must be made soon if any of these systems are to see the light of day before the year 2000. It may well be that France is arriving at the budgetary point of no return that the British reached at the end of the 1950s. But then one should never underestimate an ambitious technocracy, because critics have made the same comments at every turn of the long road the French have traveled since the mid-1950s. However, the coming budgetary crunch raises not only financial issues (how much of the GNP can the taxpayer tolerate going to defense?), or procurement problems (which weapon system for which service, or rather how many more hits can the conventional land army absorb?), but also questions of national industrial strategy.

French Industrial Policy and European Security

Since the 1940s, France has undergone an industrial revolution that arrived late but still in time to fundamentally alter the rural patterns of provincial France. This industrial transformation was to a considerable degree state-led by defense-related sectors playing a crucial role in the development of competitive high-technology industries—atomic energy, areospace and aviation, telecommunications and electronics, space satellites and launch vehicles. Today, however, doubts exist as to whether this state-led pattern of industrial development will work in the future as it has in the past.[57] One concern is that the influence of defense bureaucracies on the choice of future technology, especially that of the missile and atomic "lobbies" in the *Délégation Générale de l'Armement* (DGA) or the *Commissariat à l'Energie Atomique* (CEA) will push France in the direction of "baroque innovations" of existing technologies.[58] Another concern is that the effect of state-led modernization will distort the competitiveness of French firms in the international marketplace. Here the worry is that the influence of defense-related research and development (R&D) will perpetuate an export strategy based on "state-to-state" negotiations for big-ticket items—metro systems, or fighter aircraft—rather than a fight for position in consumer markets.

Postwar France's place in the international division of labor has been shaped by its special place in the international state system, that is, by the fact that military and industrial policies have worked together to improve her international competitive standing. The question is whether this continues to be a winning formula. Apparently, the Socialists still think so, and Mitterrand's Eureka program for the development of European-wide R&D in the sunrise industries represents an innovative variant on the traditional approach. Given the nuclear fetish of French policymakers, it seems unlikely that there is much room today for the exploration of alternative paths of development—the current fashion for neoliberal ideology notwithstanding. It is possible, however, that the space program might be a focus for reforging a technological consensus in which aerospace achievements would gradually displace the nuclear industry as France's prestige symbol. This path would not threaten the role of the state scientific and technical apparatus but it is workable only if it represents a project that can mobilize the support of other European states and their budgets. This is in effect what the Eureka project seeks to do. The fact that nearly everyone thinks of the European Space Agency's Ariane launch vehicle as a French rocket suggests that this trick is not impossible. And the fact that the Germans have signed on with budgetary support for both the Ariane 5 and the Hermès space shuttle, and the Italians and Spanish for a military version of the Spot reconnaissance satellite, suggests that the French can do it more than once.

Questions of industrial policy are relevant to understanding the promise and limits of Mitterrand's vision of France as one of the leaders of a New Europe. It is a vision in trouble because it is essentially a technocratic industrial vision of the New Europe as a commercial competitor for the United States and Japan, as well as a geopolitical power capable of rivaling Soviet influence within Central and Eastern Europe and perhaps the power of both superpowers within the Middle East. Despite the efforts of the antitotalitarian left to give this vision republican credentials and some moral depth, it is not certain that this vision of Europe has all that much appeal (or credibility) outside of the French leadership class. It does come attached to several drawbacks. Besides being wedded to a nuclear energy program that is as hazardous to economies as it is to the biosphere, it is associated with a model of state planning that appears commercially unviable. Its technocratic cast gives it the further disadvantage of not being very democratic, but it would not do to discount its appeal on those grounds alone. Despite this negative baggage, the French program has the considerable merit of clearly confronting the dangers of continued European dependence on the United States for its basic security and technological leadership without indulging in the kind of wishful thinking about the Soviet Union that leaves European pacifists open to the charge of "cooking the books."

French elites must address, all the same, what appear to be insurmountable practical and political problems if they wish to pursue substituting a European-centered security system for the American one. After all, the record shows that Europeans have had a difficult enough time deciding the question of agricultural tariffs, let alone other issues, and one can argue that U.S hegemony in Europe may well have been the precondition for what growth of European cooperation as has already been achieved.[59] In short, some observers who subscribe to a "realist" view of international cooperation believe that the U.S. security system has been critical not only for holding the Soviets at bay, but also for holding down the inter-European tensions that made the prewar European states so dangerous to one another or, more to the point, that made the Germans so dangerous to everybody else. In the absence of an alternative "hegemon" to replace the United States, further progress toward European unity seems to these analysts unlikely, and they do not hesitate to remind us that the recent European "civil wars" have been fought precisely to block the most likely candidate, the Germans, from establishing such a hegemonic position.

The recent flurry of French proposals are above all else concerned with the Germans and the political problem they may present in the coming years if the Americans ever do go home. The French vision is centered on a Franco-German partnership that will create an alternative strategic, technological, and financial pole of influence that will keep the Germans fixed in the West European orbit, and gradually attract the rest of Europe to itself, including a reluctant Great Britain. This idea is not without precedent. Certainly, progress toward greater European cooperation owes a great deal to the Franco-German couple, which has constituted the economic powerhouse of the Common Market. This is also an idea with some future. One can argue that to some degree the pole of attraction already exists—the Italians are solidly European, and the prospects have been sufficiently attractive to tempt Spain out her isolation—creating in the eyes of some French analysts new players who can help France further the European partnership whenever the Germans should hesitate.[60] These hints of a "European" dynamic that can stand alone may confirm Robert Keohane's argument that while a "hegemon" may be necessary as a guarantor while one is setting up a system of international cooperation, it may not be required once the pattern of cooperation has become the basis of long-standing arrangements.[61] The problem remains, however, that the existing pattern of European cooperation depends on the health of the Franco-German relationship and it may be that the marriage of these two central players is less radiant today than it was twenty years ago. In the last instance, the French still depend on their German partner for their vision to succeed, while the Germans may now feel free to dream again of that once and future kingdom—"Mitteleuropa."

Today's French economy is no longer the growth leader in Europe, and it is increasingly dependent on German financial and monetary support. The French have sought to offset their economic dependency by offering the Germans access to technologies that have been forbidden them—nuclear and otherwise—and an alternative channel to Moscow independent of the ups and downs of Moscow's relationship to Washington. It is not at all clear that the Germans want the technologies the French have to propose, nor is it apparent that they need additional channels to the East—they have developed their own that do well enough. Meanwhile the fact remains that Germany's fate remains hostage to the relations between the superpowers. Moscow controls access to the other half of the German nation, and Washington the security tie that steers the German defense effort and strategy. The United States simultaneously protects Germany and tries to keep her attraction towards the East in check. It is not at all clear that the end of the U.S. "protectorate" would contribute much to European solidarity, although we all might benefit in the long run if it did.

French policymakers, however, are probably right to insist that the quality of U.S. protection is deteriorating, even as the financial and strategic costs the Americans impose are going up. Unless one shares Reagan's faith in the project of restoring overall U.S. strategic superiority through SDI, the facts of Soviet-American parity and mutual vulnerability remains unavoidable, with all their consequences for the credibility of "extended deterrence" unaltered. Under conditions of parity, any U.S. promises to guarantee European security that involve that country's strategic deterrent are open to grave doubt, and any attempt to do the job with U.S. theater and battlefield forces probably inadequate. This seems to be all the more the case in view of the imminent removal of the most lethal theater weapons systems, the Pershing and cruise missiles, which involves the loss not only of nuclear warheads but the elimination of the possible deployment of conventional versions of these land-based delivery systems for future missions, such as deep interdiction strikes against second-echelon Soviet armies using "Emerging Technology" type "intelligent" munitions.

As if this gap between promise and fulfillment were not already dangerous enough, Washington during the Reagan years has fallen subject to nationalist fits and neoconservative flights in the direction of "global unilateralism." Reagan policymakers seem to have prided themselves on their disdain for European sensitivities and outlooks, and in their haste to prove themselves "not risk-adverse" have shown little restraint about putting European lives and interests in jeopardy. This combination of uncertainty and abuse may have been intended to make Europeans more attentive to American wishes,[62] but in the long run may very well contribute to making the prospect of a "creative divorce" within the Atlantic alliance thinkable, even if it is not yet feasible. The current French debate has the virtue at least of asking how the Europeans might turn such an eventuality to their own advantage rather than to that of the Soviet Union.

In any case, French elites will probably persist in trying to find another security arrangement—building the new structure within the framework of the existing alliance, drawing closer to NATO in order eventually to move farther away. Undoubtedly this internal reconstruction job will be no mean feat, but one should expect that the French will accept the challenge, if only because their vision of themselves as a power in the world will not permit them to do any less. The French persist in viewing themselves as rivals as well as clients of the U.S. superpower. The idea may strike one as either admirable or absurd, but we should admit that the program of European autonomy at least has the merit of being ambitious. Regardless of whether it makes Americans happy or not, greater European self-reliance in military as well as other areas might make everybody safer than the current arrangement based on U.S. pledges of protection that may well prove unredeemable in a crisis. The one thing that seems certain is that French elites seem agreed to pay the price of their ambitions, because, as one young French journalist declared to me: "The one thing left in the world for 'Old Europe' to conquer is Europe herself."

Notes

1. Michel Debré, "The Constitution of 1958: Its Raison d'Etre and How it Evolved," in William Andrews and Stanley Hoffmann, eds., *The Impact of the Fifth Republic on France* (Albany: State University of New York Press, 1981),

pp. 1–14. Pierre Gallois, *A Defenseless Septenate*, unpublished manuscript containing Gallois's memoirs of his conversations with de Gaulle concerning the birth of the *force de frappe*, pp. 7–9.

2. General Jeannou Lacaze, "Concept de défense et sécurité en Europe," *Revue de Défense Nationale*, June 1984, p. 17.

3. Samy Cohen, *La monarchie nucléaire* (Paris: Hachette, 1986), pp. 21–28.

4. Ministère de la Défense, *The French White Book 1972* (Paris: SIRPA, 1972).

5. See chapter 21 of Lawrence Freedman, *The Evolution of Nuclear Strategy* (New York: St. Martin's Press, 1981) for a succinct summary of this doctrine. L'Institut pour les Hautes Etudes de Défense Nationale organized annually internships for a cross-section of French civilian and military elites on defense problems that have involved thousands from different occupations over the past ten years.

6 Pascal Krop, *Les Socialistes et l'Armée* (Paris: Presses Universitaires de France, 1983), pp. 104–112.

7. Krop, *Les Socialistes et l'Armée*; Michael Harrison, "Consensus, Confusion and Confrontation: the Left in Search of a Defense Policy," in Andrews and Hoffmann, *The Impact of the Fifth Republic*, pp. 261–280.

8. See Pierre Lellouche, *L'avenir de la guerre* (Paris: Mazarine, 1985), pp. 264–278, for an intelligent dissection of the neutralist myth.

9. See David Yost, *La France et la sécurité européenne* (Paris: Presses Universitaires de France, 1985), pp. 36–45; 229–257. (English edition: *France's Deterrent Posture and Security in Europe* [London: International Institute of Strategic Studies, 1985]).

10. Thierry de Montbrial and Régis Debray, "Quelle politique étrangère pour la France?" *Le Débat*, No. 34 (March 1985), p. 43.

11. Dominique Moïsi used this expression in his introduction to the summer issue of *Politique Internationale*, No. 2 (1985), p. 317.

12. This was a theme that came up often during my interviewing in Paris in 1985 and 1986. My French informants seemed very skeptical about Great Britain's right to make a similar claim, on the grounds that Great Britain depends on the United States for its delivery systems, on U.S. testing facilities and technology for the development of its nuclear warheads and guidance systems, and is subject to U.S. oversight and control over any British initiatives in sharing her nuclear technology with third parties. The fact of British dependency is inscribed in the limits of Britain's national technology, and does not only follow from the formal integration of British Nuclear Forces with U.S. forces in a common targeting plan, the SIOP.

13. The formula "nuclear nationalism" is Diane Johnstone's, whose book, *The Politics of Euromissiles*, (New York: Schocken Books, 1985), has an interesting chapter on France.

14. Dick Howard, "French Foreign Policy: An Interview with Pierre Hassner and Patrick Viveret," *Telos*, No. 55 (1983), pp. 227–228.

15. Krop, *Les Socialistes et l'Armée*, pp. 104–112.

16. Ibid., p. 109.

17. Interviews with participants, Paris, 1985.

18. Krop, *Les Socialistes et l'Armée*, pp. 64–71; Nancy Lieber, "French Socialist Foreign Policy: Atlantic Relations, Defense and European Unity," in Bogdan Denitch, ed., *Democratic Socialism* (Montclair, N.J.: Allenheld & Osmun, 1981), p. 122.

19. Krop, *Les Socialistes et l'Armée*, p. 134, footnote 19.

20. This is based on my interview with a former senior official of the Foundation pour les Etudes de Défense Nationale (F.E.D.N.) in the spring of 1985.

21. Krop, *Les Socialistes et l'Armée*, p. 107.

22. Ibid., p. 108.

23. Ibid., p. 107.

24. Ibid., p. 97.

25. Ibid., pp. 15–24.

26. Charles Hernu, *Nous les Grands* (Paris: F.G.-France, 1980), p. 63.

27. Nicole Gnesotto, "PC, PS: une ligne peut en cacher une autre," *Esprit*, No. 79 (July 1983), p. 89.

28. This is based on my 1985 interview with party defense analysts, but also see Luc Rosenweig, "La politique extérieure, un domaine en friche," *Le Monde*, 2 April 1987, p. 9.

29. Gnesotto, "PC, PS...," p. 88.

30. Harlem Désir is a member of the PS and has been groomed as a possible candidate.

31. See François Mitterrand's comments opposing any modification of French tactical doctrines and his endorsement of the INF accord in his "Lettre à tous les Français," advertising insert, *Libération*, 7 April 1988, p. 11, and the transcript of his televised debate with Jacques Chirac, *Libération*, 30 April 1988, pp. 10–11.

32. See Diana Pinto's "La conversion de l'intelligentsia," in Dennis Lacorne, Jacques Rupnik, and Marie-France Toinet, eds., *L'Amérique dans les têtes* (Paris: Hachette, 1986), pp. 102–108.

33. Cornelius Castoriadis, "The Social Regime in Russia," *Telos*, No. 38 (Winter 1978/79), pp. 36–37, and his interview, "Le plus dur et le plus fragile des régimes," *Esprit*, No. 63 (1982), p. 140.

34. Paul Thibaud, "Mesure d'une défaite," *Esprit*, No. 63 (March 1982), pp. 108–109, and also his introduction to the special issue "Devant les totalitarismes," *Esprit*, No. 64 (April 1982), pp. 3–10.

35. André Glucksman, "Le pacifisme en Europe," *Esprit*, No. 67–68 (1982), pp. 14–20.

36. Jacques Rupnik and Muriel Humbertjean, "Images des Etats-Unis dans l'opinion publique," in Lacorne, Rupnik, and Toinet, *L'Amérique dans les têtes*.

37. Paul Thibaud, "Les évêques américains entre la guerre juste et le pacifisme," *Esprit*, No. 79 (1983), p. 97.

38. Paul Thibaud, "Politique internationale: principe et stratégie," *Esprit*, No. 58 (1981), pp. 75–80.

39. Gregory Flynn, "Opinions publiques et mouvements pacifistes," in Pierre Lellouche, ed., *Dissuasion et pacifisme* (Paris: Institut Français des Relations Internationales, 1982), pp. 223–237.

40. Paul Thibaud, "Pacifism and its Problems," *Telos*, No. 59 (1984), pp. 152–164.

41. See Lellouche, *l'avenir de la guerre*, p. 21.

42. See Pierre Lellouche, "France and the Euromissiles," *Foreign Affairs* 62, No. 2 (Winter 1983/84), pp. 318–333; see also Dominique Moïsi, "Les limites du consensus," in Lellouche, *Dissuasion et pacifisme*.

43. Thibaud, "Pacifism and its Problems."

44. Michel Martin, *From Warriors to Managers* (Chapel Hill: University of

North Carolina Press, 1981), pp. 158–159.

45. See Diane Johnstone's report on West German opinion polls, *In These Times*, 21 May 1986, p. 11.

46. See Charles Hernu's declaration in *Le Monde*, 22 June, 1985, p. 1.

47. See Yost,, *La France et la sécurité européenne*, pp. 162–177.

48. General Gallois, "Le mythe de la défense européenne," in *L'Allemagne et L'avenir de l'Europe* (Paris: Anthropos, 1984), p. 155; see also Gérard Fuchs's reply from a Socialist perspective in the same volume.

49. Jean-Yves Boulic, "La bombe à neutrons française est `prête'," *Le Point*, 17 November 1986, p. 32.

50. Rumor about the production of neutron weapons were already in circulation in Paris in the summer of 1985. Some French parliamentarians have expressed to me their frustration with the government's policy of pursuing the development of these weapons while refusing to announce to France's allies and her own public that their production had already begun.

51. Pierre Lellouche created quite a a scandal when he proposed this for the first time in the spring of 1985 in the conclusion of his book *L'avenir de la guerre*. Since that time his call has been picked up by other personalities on the right.

52. See Diane Johnstone's portrait of the Juquin campaign in *In These Times*, 11–17 November 1987, p. 11, and *Le Monde*, 10 April, 1987, p. 10.

53. The nuclear share of equipment expenditure in the past four-year defense program is 31 percent or 131.5 billion francs, which at current exchange rates works out to about 19 billion dollars for the life of the program, or a yearly average of around 4.7 billion dollars, substantially less that the Reagan budgetary request for the Strategic Defense Initiative in 1987.

54. *Le Monde*, 28 June 1985, p. 1.

55. This was the tone of much of the right's criticism in the spring and summer of 1986.

56. The Foundation for National Defense Studies (F.E.D.N.) was officially charged in the fall of 1986 with the task of coming up with a response to the gradual infiltration of hostile propaganda into the French Press.

57. See Hugo Sada, "Un marché tendu," and "La France face à ses armes," in *Armes: France 3ème Grand*, published by *Autrement* (Oct. 1985), pp. 178–179. Also, many of these themes came up in interviewing I did in the summer of 1986.

58. I owe much of this argument to Mary Kaldor's *Baroque Arsenal* (New York: Hill & Wang, 1981), but I heard echoes of this position from both members of CODENE and some French defense specialists in interviews done in 1985.

59. This point is developed by Josef Joffe, "The Cost of Abandoning Europe," *The National Interest* 1, No. 3 (Spring 1987), pp. 33–39.

60. See François Heisbourg's article "Défense française: l'impossible statu quo," *Politique Internationale*, No. 36 (Summer 1987), p. 141.

61. See Robert O. Keohane, *After Hegemony* (Princeton: Princeton University Press, 1984), ch. 3.

62. See "The Uncertainty Principle," by Owen Harris, which discusses the utility of playing on the "insecurity" of the allies, in *The National Interest* 1, No. 2 (1985).

CHAPTER 4

A Neighbor's Fears: Enduring Issues in Franco-German Relations

ANDRÉ BRIGOT

Although the importance of Franco-German relations runs like a leitmotif in the French political discourse on security and defense issues, there is a striking gap between emphatic declarations and feeble achievements. The affective or symbolic terms like "shared destiny," Franco-German "coupling" or "friendship," and the "need to overcome historical antagonisms," frequently used at the closing of bilateral meetings, mitigate the slim measures actually adopted.

As if to escape this *trompe l'oeil*, several proposals have been put forward, especially on the French side. They range from mutual consultations or studies which, at the top levels of governments, strive to dissipate strategic oppositions, to specific measures that are too limited to promote broader cooperation.

This chapter examines the elements and mechanisms that form the basis of different analyses of the security questions facing the two countries. They include cultural differences which define collective images, differences of global strategy which help understand positions and institutions, as well as differing approaches to current problems leading to responses that are at best individualistic and at worst incompatible. Far from promoting skepticism, this chapter will probe the conditions that may lead toward progress in Franco-German relations. However, rather than define a supposedly common objective, we shall reflect on the reciprocal identity of the two protagonists, assuming that the identity of each must first be strengthened before the two can transcend their objectively distinct situations. Beyond the development of an argument, we hope that by shedding light on mutual perceptions our own French discourse can be adapted to German concerns.

The Cultural Framework

Through the Eyes of the Sovereign

France is very lucky. She is, or believes herself to be, "sovereign"—not independent or autarkic, but possessing great decisionmaking autonomy, however economically, technically, scientifically, or historically dependent she may be.

Many elements reassure France in this image of herself. Hexagonal in shape, she sees herself centered on her almost centrally located capital. She is approaching the bicentennial of her Revolution after having gradually granted the president of the Republic attributes of a sovereign. She regularly affords herself the increasingly costly luxury of opposing one or the other of the two superpowers at the risk of reinforcing her neighbors' image of herself as a leader without means.

Deeply influenced by this centuries-old identity, the French ill imagine that the Germans might see themselves totally differently, or at least that they do not aspire to develop, reestablish, or follow that model. Nor can they conceive that a country may have been only briefly unified, have a capital city where power has never been completely centralized, that the national referent might be to people (the Germans) with the political will to live on a certain territory rather than to the territory itself (France), or that the German sense of community might rest essentially on language.

The French assume that other countries function along lines similar to their own. As far as Germany is concerned, they both expect and fear this eventuality, hence the constant worry about "German reunification." Convinced that it can be the only major and immediate objective of the Germans (which, if it were achieved, would be catastrophic for France, with the new economic threat replacing the former military one), the French are forever watchful of manifestations of this hidden goal. They face a West Germany that willingly keeps a low profile, minimizes its advantages, does not advertise its interests, and avoids publicly opposing her allies' initiatives. Consequently, the French interpret any slightly unusual German action as proof positive of that infamous wish for reunification. Territorial unity and sovereignty being integral to the French political consciousness, they find it difficult to fathom the implications of a divided territory and to believe in the Germans' acceptance of a long process of evolution. Thus, some Frenchmen who believe themselves to be keen strategists denounce a reunification plot behind the smallest opening to the East, pointing to such self-evident process as "reunification through neutralization."

If the Germans respond that the reunification question is not appropriate, then they must be deceitful. Some of them point out that other countries, more powerful than France, fear and would oppose this eventuality: France does not have to be the first to pay the price for this dubious battle. But it is as if it were important that the French themselves carry the burden of denouncing and rejecting. It is as if we alone were entrusted to come up with very cutting answers to a problem we do not even conceptualize well.

Remembered Fears

Regarding security issues, one must examine the mutual fears and traumas that color French perceptions. Beyond objective threats (e.g., the assessment of potential military forces), how can one grasp the collective worries that, today, structure the political discourse and in a crisis would constitute real vulnerabilities?

As a whole, France does not have a collective memory of destruction comparable to Germany's. If there is a lasting trauma, it comes less from having seen the sudden collapse of the strongest military force of its time than from the establishment of a legal political collaboration that was unique in Europe. The shameful act, redeemed by de Gaulle, was not to have lost, but to have compromised political sovereignty during the Occupation. Likewise, the reference to "Munich" as a reminder of cowardice still influences the French political vocabulary, while remaining meaningless in West Germany.

It seems that Germany, which has suffered the two steps toward the loss of national identity (material destruction and political occupation), reacts differently. On the one hand, she finds occupation a lesser evil: one powerful protector and several lesser ones saved the Germans from an even greater servitude in 1945. On the other hand, do not contemporary worries originate in the memory of material destruction and of the interwar economic ruin? Does not the idea of being *the* potential battlefield lead to the fear of nuclear weapons that would bring the most unimaginable destruction?

No doubt one fears less the unfamiliar or unimagined. Lacking a collective memory of the ravages of war, France can threaten by risking its own existence, even in order to preserve its sovereignty. West Germany, which was saved by occupation (but at a continuing political cost), can only fear that which endangers what she has left: a reduced territory—all the more so since she could not control the decision to use nuclear weapons. Therein perhaps originates the lack of appeal of conventional forces for the French. They are ready to use nuclear threats because they cannot forever be retreating to the Marne or to the North Sea. Conversely, they do not fully understand that basing deterrence on the ultimate threat may be considered dangerous and imprudent.

By asserting that a conflict in Europe, even one conventional battle, would lead inevitably to nuclear warfare, many French think they are "rationally" guaranteeing peace. Among them, we must include those who for some thirty years have developed the instruments, the weapons systems, and the appropriate discourse of minimal nuclear deterrence. Albeit imperfect locally, it seems more coherent at the global level than any conventional deterrence.

Although this discourse has been adopted by several successive political leaders, there remain many skeptics or opponents. Some criticize nuclear weapons as a symbol of militarization. Others reject them on the ground that they foreclose "battles," which are the true tests of strength. War-fighting still retains supporters, or at least prophets, who are ever ready to start tearing down the nuclear walls in the name of realism.

Many "unnatural" alliances thus come into being. For example, in Germany and in France there are those who share the rejection of any type of conflict, although they use opposite strategies: reliance on the nuclear threat for some, denuclearization as the first step toward disarmament for others. Alliances may be forged between the "tactical" opponents of nuclear weapons and those who wish to do away with nuclear weapons so as to better rebuild a "conventional deterrence" based on an enormous modernization of conventional weapons. It is a grave error to think that all antinuclear activists, in France as elsewhere, are pacifists. The United States, for example, can preach both a more offense-oriented conventional strategy and, at the same time, limitations on nuclear weapons.

Unfortunately, the rational defense of the nuclear strategy cannot affect West Germany which itself seeks limits on nuclear escalation instead of a French nuclear guarantee. The Germans seem to be paralyzed by their perception of the risks, whereas the French have but an abstract vision of the danger. For the first time in French history, the enemy is not at the border. Moreover, we cannot imagine that we might become a stake in a conflict, nor in what way we might be threatened.[1]

It is difficult for the French to understand how weary the Germans are of the numerous troops stationed and maneuvering on their soil. With half the soldiers and twice the area, the "military" is acceptable in France where the soldiers are French soldiers under national authority. What is more, the French do not really think of themselves or their country as "targets," perhaps the result of their internalizing a nuclear logic that denies that any political goal can be achieved by war.

It is equally difficult for the French to realize how worried the Germans are about environmental destruction. Thousands of hectares of forest burn down each summer in France without causing a psychological shock comparable to that caused by acid rain in Germany. Twenty years of nuclear power plants, the result of a national nuclear venture (from the mythology of the prewar atomic scientists to the progressive establishment of a nuclear arsenal) have, despite ironical and disbelieving comments, immunized the French against the fears of a nuclear accident. Fears have been largely defused by letting the centralized political authority handle the responsibilities and worries associated with environmental protection. The risks are presumed to be dealt with by the experts, hence the French insensitivity and surprise toward environmental concerns and toward the social movements that express them. The French understand perfectly well the "Greens'" distrust of politicians, but not of a supposedly competent bureaucracy.

The French see these misgivings about technology and the rejection of the consequences of growth as coming from a privileged country. Compared to unemployment and deindustrialization, many ecological themes are considered secondary concerns to be dealt with in the future. Alarmist rhetoric in France has been defused by the vague idea that new technologies could be a source of employment and by a less visibly damaged environment.

Finally, the intellectual links between ecology and pacifism are not clearly drawn. The groups that support these objectives are more separated in France than in Germany. Whereas German groups have often expressed their reservations or their criticisms with confidence, and sometimes with a strong sectarianism, in France such criticisms have at best been weak, and at worst gone in the opposite direction. It was not difficult to make the French understand the reservations of a great many Germans about the military situation of West Germany and their questioning of NATO. But these criticisms have only been perceived as a rejection of *all* forms of military security. The little research done on alternative formulas does not seem to have received any real expression in France, hence the often dishonest use of German slogans like "better red than dead" to countenance the rationale of those who denounce reunification and promote the speedy creation of a Franco-German army.

Yet, and this is a new aspect of this country's politics, the French feel truly affected by, and committed to, the security of Germany. Although confirmed by all the recent opinion polls, this observation of course does not by itself constitute a guarantee. The French understand or perceive poorly the risks weighing on Germany. For the last ten years, public opinion has reflected anti-Soviet currents that bring together diverse movements, be they liberal, antitotalitarian, or against the lyricism of 1968. All this can change, however.

But all French politicians, with the exception of the Communists, consider the development of a common European military security, particularly in cooperation with West Germany, as fundamental. This appears to reflect a real change of perspective that West German leaders, secure in their traditional image of a selfish and haughty France, have not sufficiently taken into account.

French and German Security Strategies

Although Germany is no longer perceived to be a military threat, concerns have appeared in other areas. Let us discuss economics first.

The Economic Gap

Gone are the hopes of equal French and German gross domestic products, much less of equal balances of trade.[2] The gap keeps widening through the years. It is more and more in the minds of leaders, while the man in the street finds German goods superior to the French or at least endowed with more solid qualities (for example, in automobiles, household appliances, and manufacturing). Thus, economic rather than military might is now feared, which stirs up the usual and often irrational feelings of inferiority.

Curiously enough, French public opinion has not denounced German farm subsidies. On the other hand, one is surprised that West Germany does not more openly support French technological gambles in space, aeronautics, or, earlier, in nuclear research. There are two conflicting traditions here: the German one dominated by concerns over profits, and the French one more eager to launch into technological ventures whatever their commercial possibilities. But the widening gap between French and German production levels has a serious impact on security projects. Does not cooperation between the two countries presuppose a balance of power, beyond their complementary aspects which can certainly be of great use?

Since the existence of nuclear weapons imposes great limitations on any "sharing," as we shall see, proposals for cooperation focus on conventional forces. The defense of Germany, based on large manpower, is handicapped by a demographic decline. It would be unhealthy were Franco-German cooperation to take the form of buying French "mercenaries" more or less equipped through the West German budget. The allocation of duties between overly unequal states consciously or unconsciously arouses reservations and reticence. One cannot hold her economic success against West Germany. Nor can one think that an economically inferior country could embark on a defense cooperation with a stronger neighbor without running some risks.

The Demographic Question

Another divergence between French and German sensitivities stems from the Germans' unconcern about evolving demographic rates. If the birth rate remains at the current level (in West Germany, an average of 1.4 children per woman since 1974; 1.2 for native Germans), and the death rate and immigration/emigration ratio do not change much, the Federal Republic could have fewer people than France by the end of the century. If the trend continues, the population of the two Germanies could fall below the French within fifty years (see Table 1).

Table 1. Evolution of the Population of the Federal Republic of Germany (FRG), the German Democratic Republic (GDR), and France (in millions).

	FRG	GDR	France
1975	62	17	53
1985	61	17	55
2025	45	14	55

Source: Klaus Peter Möller, "Überalterung der Bevölkerung in der BRD," *Universitas* 40 (1985), pp.1003-1013.

The military started feeling the effects of this declining birth rate as early as 1985 and will do so increasingly until 1991. In the labor market, the number of new entries is now beginning to decrease and will do so more markedly until the next decade when it will be fairly weak. This leads to the possibility of the disappearance of unemployment.

But as a central constituent of Europe, is Germany going to contribute to its decline or weakening? Will the situation give rise to new opportunities for pressure? For example, the falling population of West Germany eliminates the possibilities of emigration to Berlin. If current population trends persist, Berlin's population could fall from two million around 1980 to eight hundred thousand around 2040. Beyond a certain point, Berlin's population could shrink geometrically and the resulting feeling of insecurity engender mass departures. Although a few leaders are aware of the situation, a certain taboo remains intact: it is still impossible to talk about the demography of the Federal Republic without bringing up images of Nazism.

The effects of this demographic situation can be viewed from different perspectives. On the one hand, as far as the balance *within* Europe is concerned, the situation is theoretically favorable to France. At the beginning of the next millenium, the population balance will be tipped in our favor, which again diminishes the threat of the possible reunification of the two Germanies. On the other hand, if one considers Europe in its global context, the German situation keenly accentuates its aging and fragility, especially since the process of integrating non-European populations, whose relative weight will increase, seems to be much weaker and less polished in German society than in French society.

The Gift of Time: The "Glacis"

West Germany unwillingly gives us some time. Thanks to its geographical position, German territory puts several hundred kilometers between us and the potential enemy. German readers have already thought of the "glacis." Are they right?

The French did not force West Germany to contribute to France's security in this way, and it is fallacious to argue that French doctrine treats German territory only as a maneuvering area, if not a battlefield. This territory also gives decisionmakers time needed for crisis management. It will enable decisionmakers to react, maneuver, and (in France) to postpone the threat of using strategic nuclear forces. German territory adds to this time, and any force reduction in Central Europe that would increase the rapidity of an offense can only worry us. This does not mean that we applaud any excessive arms buildup in West Germany, nor is it up to us to decide the appropriate force levels within the strategy of flexible response. However, any disarmament process that would reduce this time would leave us with none other than the nuclear option.

This need for time is the fault line of a defensive strategy. In West Germany, the idea of stopping an invasion as early as possible and at the lowest possible level, or of preventing misperceptions and a surprise attack through confidence-building measures, stems from the same logic: the need to gain time. We know quite well, both in France and in West Germany, that we have precious little time, particularly due to the technical shortening of the time available for retaliation. Although they take different forms in the two countries, the political effects of this situation share similar characteristics. Since retaliation should be almost instantaneous, or to put it simply, since we are approaching automaticity, both countries confront the same time problem. However, if one contemplates a slow progression of enemy forces across Germany, then Germany is indeed a "glacis." If, on the other hand, even a conventional attack must be detected, assessed, and met with lightning speed by both West Germany and France, then Germany is less a "glacis" than a field of action that becomes crucial given developments in C3 technology (control, command, communication).

We do not wish here to dismiss the reality of a stronger threat on German territory. Rather, we would like to think of German territory not in terms of its objective military usefulness, but as another area subject to the same time constraints whose technological aspects require a common political response.

Hidden Behind Siegfried?

The Federal Republic has the strongest concentration of conventional and nuclear forces in Europe, and perhaps in the world. This situation, which she would gladly do without, results both from geography and from the outcome of World War II. France benefits from this situation because not only is the enemy not at her borders, but considerable military forces confront it.

The conventional French presence. Yet, as a member of the Atlantic alliance, France participates concretely in this military presence. This may of course be considered a failure, since forty years of French troops in Germany have not led to any major movement toward greater understanding and cooperation. But the French are sometimes surprised by the constant denunciations of their national "selfishness" when, in peacetime, more than 10 percent of the total French forces are stationed in Germany, namely the Berlin Brigade and the Second Corps at Baden-Baden (which is directly supported by the First and Third Corps based at Metz and Lille and with which it constitutes the First Army). Supported by the Tactical Air Force, the Mechanized Air Forces represent, on a war footing, about 350,000 men, 1,100 tanks, and about 300 planes, spearheaded or supported by the 47,000 men of the Rapid Action Force (FAR), and more particularly by its division of antitank helicopters. Since they are already linked, these forces can be very quickly regrouped for counterattack in Germany, the heart of NATO's Central European command, without having to cross an ocean or sea. This contribution, which easily bears comparison to that of other members of NATO, should spare us this type of criticism.

Although German doctrine emphasizes forward defense, it corresponds historically to an offensive strategy. The more West Germany tries to develop a defensive attitude within the context of détente and confidence-building measures in Europe, the more she will need depth, that is, to include French territory if only conceptually. Considered today as "reserve territory" by NATO and the *Bundeswehr*, this area conversely extends beyond the Rhine for the First Army since it is a forward tactical zone. Without denying the notion of national borders, these facts, more than legal formalizations, should place in context the widespread German image of a France withdrawn well behind the Rhine and her nuclear weapons. Most soldiers and many politicians, on both sides of the Rhine, know of the reality of this French presence, its importance in case hostilities break out, and its *inevitable* participation in any future conflict. But this reality faces a double taboo.

In West Germany, it is as if recognizing this fact involved the risk of minimizing the fundamental U.S. guarantee through some implicit and derisory substitution. Moreover, German legalism is uncomfortable with unspoken agreements that might prove meaningless because of French reservations concerning her independent and free decision to defend her ally should the occasion arise. This is, however, a strange impression when one considers that the commitments of other countries are not any clearer, and that French forces are on the European continent, as opposed to the greater part of U.S. and British forces whose arrival would remain problematic in a time of crisis. Although France may benefit from the German military barrier, neither ocean nor sea separates her from the potential enemy.

It seems that politicians in France considered the political situation that existed when she withdrew from the integrated military command to be immutable, and that it was dangerous to state clearly the extent and the details of our military contribution to the alliance. It is difficult to assess the relevance of these reservations. French public opinion seems to have become more favorable to concrete and specific expressions of her solidarity with her neighbors. Must we lose the political benefit of our concrete commitments by keeping them quiet? Rather than being regularly accused of selfishness, would it not be better to be explicit about the true situation, including its implications and its limits, especially since the processes on which West Germany relies are unclear? For example, although U.S. troops are certainly needed for combat operations, they are above all "hostages," since one cannot imagine their annihilation without some American response from the United States' own territory. Other allies who are never accused of being selfish appear poorly prepared for a sustained effort should the situation arise. Although often involved in external operations less vital for them than Central Europe, it is the French who have assumed a forward position since they are in Berlin, have the second largest military force on the potential battlefield along with the only de facto reserves, and yet who seem to be forever considered untrustworthy.

Could we not be viewed as an integral part of this common military barrier? And within it, do we have the right to comment on its evolution? Instead of talking about "defending the national sanctuary," should we not be taking into account our de facto contribution to the security of West Germany?

The need for nuclear weapons. The French thus wonder about the consequences, both military (in times of crisis) and political (in peacetime) of a process of European denuclearization. In fact, there is no doubt that in a denuclearized Europe, France would appear as if endowed with a major potential military capacity that would make her *the only* continental nuclear power. Members of the Warsaw Pact led by the USSR would, of course, denounce this situation as dangerous if not warlike.

But we also know that the United States has never gladly accepted that nuclear strategic forces give France the means of threatening to use nuclear weapons and trigger a process that the two superpowers could not control. As long as these strategic weapons are not integrated into NATO's planning groups, that is, as long as French decisionmakers have the means of interfering with the game the two superpowers play, of "breaking the condominium," no one knows where a conflict in Europe in which France would be forced to participate would lead.

This situation, which contributes to France's international power and which other countries understand and have adapted (e.g., China), would be challenged if France were the only European nuclear power. Concerns do not originate so much in the perspective of a reduction of nuclear arsenals, which we can only applaud, than from having to justify constantly a defense strategy centered on nuclear deterrence. International public opinion would accuse us of increasing risks. More insidious criticisms from governments would tend to extract concessions from us in exchange for their tacit support. Then, should France withdraw behind her autonomous nuclear forces, or put this insignificant addition at the disposal of NATO's integrated command?

French nuclear weapons compensate for a massive conventional inferiority in Europe. If we were to sacrifice them, and if the Warsaw Pact retained its superiority in conventional weapons, then we would have to launch a costly and not too convincing conventional arms buildup. It is therefore only if a double process of nuclear and *conventional* disarmament were set into motion that we could start on the same path without apprehension. But this double-zero option is nowhere in sight.

Uncertainty and Predictability

Another factor explains the French reservations toward the process of European denuclearization, and its effects are felt in quite a few other areas of Franco-German security relations. West Germany wants to be "computable" (*berechnenbar*). Having provoked two or three wars with her neighbors in the last century, Germany wants to be predictable and reassuring. The fears that others could have of Germany demonstrates this concern. In defense matters, West Germany supports confidence-building measures, early notification of maneuvers, and seeks in every way to alleviate other countries' fears of surprise of any sort, especially military. Likewise, one should be able to predict commitments in times of crisis or war, and to know the processes involved and their development, not only out of a concern for efficiency but also in order to control their sequence and precisely handle escalation.

On the other hand, unpredictability is one of the major intellectual foundations of French strategic doctrine. French retaliation, in order to deter (that is, so as not to be used), relies on the enemy's *inability to predict* whether French conventional and especially nuclear forces will actually be used, and if so where, when, and for what. This is as true of the air-to-ground capabilities of the FAR, whose mobility is one of its strengths, as of the ever-undefined threshold beyond which the decisionmaker will use strategic nuclear weapons.

When a few German leaders ask the French to participate in integrated nuclear target planning, not only does it raise questions about sovereignty and reintegration into NATO, it also challenges one of the bases of deterrence. The more unpredictable we are, the more complex the enemy's calculations and decision to take a risk. Up to a point, the more variables included in a deterrence system, the more difficult calculations become. Thus, the military function of "pre-strategic" nuclear weapons is not only to force a dispersion of enemy tank forces. They also compel the enemy to take an additional variable into account in the rational calculations governing his decision to attack: where, when, and how many of these weapons would be used, independent from NATO, to achieve what national objective?

This explains why these two peoples talk past each other, with the Germans multiplying their demands for "predictability" and the French apparently dodging them and being accused again of holy egoism when what they consider fundamental is asked to be shared. But there is a distinction between the *inevitability* of our commitment, which should make us reassuring and predictable, and the *uncertainty* for the enemy as to the nature, time, and location of that commitment.

Perhaps this confusion arises from the German fears of both their enemy's and allies' weapons. Certainly, our friend's territory must not be a free-fire zone. But the same friend should not alternatively claim that French forces are insufficiently shared when referring to the threat posed by the Warsaw Pact, and also judge them dangerous in and of themselves without considering their justification and their *raison d'être*. Or else, that friend ought to tell us the best way to achieve the dual objective of putting off the threat while limiting destruction. If these two goals are linked, can we say for certain that nuclear weapons do not have some advantages over conventional ones, even if the latter were modernized?

Current Questions

A Fear of Disarmament?

Should we not fear a nuclear-free Germany rather than its far-off reunification? We shall use this idea as the application to the Federal Republic of a general movement toward European denuclearization and not as the political goal of Germany only, even though it is popular.

This movement is hoped for by quite diverse groups. Mr. Gorbachev made it a goal for the next century. Others see it as a way to achieve peace. No one can reasonably criticize the current reduction of nuclear arsenals. What a marvelous consensual theme launched by leaders touched by the grace of God! Of course, this will not be achieved soon or even in the medium term (because of verification obstacles), but it looms over the horizon of European security.

In order to understand the French position on this matter, we must remember that the French strategy of nuclear deterrence does not rest on the concept of equilibrium. We do not try to be as strong as the USSR. Rather, we try to deter through our ability to inflict worse destruction than whatever she could hope to gain, or, at the very least, to weaken her seriously and leave her to face the undamaged United States. To be believable, this threat does not have to be of the same nature or quantity as that of the potential aggressor. It only requires technological credibility (the ability to penetrate and reach targets) and politico-psychological credibility (that the opponent believes that the French decisionmakers would fire nuclear weapons, whatever may be the national or international pressures, or even the future of France).

Would this credibility hold under a zero- or a double-zero option? The current proposals leave such a gap between French forces and the arsenals of the two superpowers that reducing them by 50 percent or even more would not give France any superiority, nor could it grant her the capacity to launch preemptive strikes. As for tactical nuclear weapons, French nuclear capacities that are certainly disquieting for anyone living in Germany, would not actually be used except in conjunction with our allies' nuclear forces (i.e., U.S.), unless they are withdrawn or taken. In other words, the additional destruction would probably have only marginal effects.

Who Benefits from the Negotiations?

French strategic doctrine explains in part the intellectual separation between the organization of the defense of the country and the arms control process. Whereas in West Germany the notion of security includes defense *and* détente, and whereas progress toward détente implies tangible results for the German public (better travel conditions between East and West, especially by politicians and divided families, and better trade and economic relations), nothing concrete can generally follow a French agreement with the East. The French are not very sensitive to the commercial dimension of international relations. Instead, they express the political dimension of dominance relationships better than their human consequences for the division of the Germans.

Hence the lack of understanding, if not the suspiciousness, of the German insistence on establishing and maintaining a climate of trust with the USSR. Since the superpowers have for several years been the only source of tensions as well as détente, the French collective perception of the negotiations and their usefulness fluctuates between indifference and distrust. All the more so since a declining French Communist party has unfortunately become the main disseminator of pacifist arguments and of Gorbachev's policies, which it makes immediately suspicious.

As far as their security interests are concerned, the French do not need change in Europe; or, to be less contentious, they do not perceive the links between these developments and their own collective or individual interests. This does not mean that the latter do not exist, or that the French are indifferent to any improvement in the situation in Central Europe. France has contributed to the success of the Conference on Security and Cooperation in Europe and to the establishment of confidence-building measures. She is also sensitive to the situation in Czechoslovakia, Poland, and elsewhere.

Concerns that have a strong meaning for the Germans do not, on the face of it, affect the French doctrine of minimal deterrence since it is from the outset what a weaker country relies upon against a stronger power. We cannot work toward a "defense-oriented" posture rather than develop offense-oriented means: we have felt defense-oriented for nearly two centuries in Europe. The idea that an attack could "start from French soil," to parody a German phrase, is for us ridiculous and unthinkable. Here again, the Germans must understand that nuclear weapons have their own logic. Our attitude toward the East is devoid of any guilt feeling or of any quest for reconciliation. Militarily-speaking, the image of the USSR as a potential aggressor is recent, unclear, and contradicted by a history of alliances. There is no reason, in any case, to adopt a low profile in these relations.

Thus, the French tend to see in negotiations born mostly of non-European initiatives only the nefarious consequences that they could have on the French security organization. We are more eager to prevent the deployment of an ABM system which will reduce Soviet vulnerability to our strategic missiles than to seek the elimination of nuclear weapons in Europe that would leave untouched the missiles that threaten us. Facing the obscure debates over weapons of different ranges, there remains the simple idea that "he who can do the most can do the least." As long as the USSR has long-range nuclear weapons, our vulnerability and our strategic situation will change little.

Before assessing the current negotiations, the question then becomes: can France and Germany have a common Eastern policy? Are our interests similar, and can our perceptions and objectives move closer to each other? For example, do we share the same concept of conventional arms control?

On the other hand, this concern for Central Europe, although of prime importance to the two countries, should not let us forget that France has interests and commitments outside Europe. Some critics see them only as the remnants of a prior era. France must assess the value of this heritage and examine its cost and function. But the lack of understanding, if not the ironic attitude, of a great many Germans about French actions or interests outside Europe cannot be productive. Although the French must understand the interests and concerns of the Germans, the Germans cannot be uninterested or ironic about ours. Any European foreign policy will have to take these factors into account.

The lack of understanding of the other country's problems may not imply fear of its activities, but is always the basis from which indifference or distrust develops. One aspect of this distrust is expressed in France by the idea that one must do something with West Germany to keep her from falling toward the East. Although honesty forces us to express so coarsely an idea common among certain French leaders, it would be dramatic for people in the Federal Republic, however, to think that this idea alone lies behind French invitations (often confused and disparate to be sure) to organize our mutual solidarity and security. On the contrary, the dominant feeling is that any violation of the integrity of West Germany would constitute a major threat for France. We support Germany because we fear for ourselves far more than we fear her Eastern policy.

Before examining the proposals discussed in France, one must mention a new grievance felt by the French: we do not know what the Germans want. To be sure, French proposals or speeches are often easy to criticize, unrealistic, or even pretentious. But what can the French offer the Germans when the latter are asking what they themselves know the French cannot give, or, to put it more kindly, when they appear to not even know what they want or what they are offering? What form can a Franco-German dialogue take when the one partner neither has, nor wants to have, its own strategy? We do realize that West Germany is limited to NATO's strategy, and we will not question that here. But we also know that this strategy does not meet all of Germany's concerns. The absence of German strategic thinking for more than forty years is surprising. The point is not to deny the links with the Nazi period that exist in this area as in others. But the disappearance of such thought is just as worrisome and makes it hard for our two countries to work together (unless West Germany finds it more convenient not to have any strategy!).

Further, the French military is less and less knowledgeable about West Germany. Before 1939, our potential opponent was German, so our officers learned to speak German and knew at least something about German thought. Today, the Soviets are the opponent, and the Germans have become allies whom we still know and understand poorly. This reduced knowledge only strengthens the monopoly held by a small group of French authors and experts whose ideas about German issues hardly differ any more.

What proposals are there? The French proposals for increased security cooperation can be approached from a dual perspective. The political perspective pits those who see France's pulling out of NATO's integrated military command as useless and no longer valid, against those who hope both to maintain the freedom of action it has given, and to help Germany and Europe benefit from that very freedom. The military perspective concerns the possibility of cooperation on nuclear and conventional arms.

The Atlanticist old guard certainly seems to be the most generous. Not only would they allow conventional French troops to occupy a "crenel" in the allied forward defense, but since deep down they do not believe in the French doctrine of strategic deterrence, they would be willing to deploy more pre-strategic nuclear forces and integrate them into a defense barrier. Hardly sensitive to the German fears of nuclear weapons, and as long as there exists no credible military alternative to using nuclear weapons to compensate for conventional imbalances in Europe, they see a major advantage in giving a nuclear dimension to Franco-German solidarity, to wit, a more widespread acceptance of nuclear weapons if France were not the only one to possess them and even if she had to share the decision to use them.

Regarding West Germany, this position may satisfy those who are forever asking France to rejoin NATO and to occupy a "crenel." It does not, however, resolve German fears concerning NATO's strategy and its military organization. Will one more worried member be enough to Europeanize the way NATO operates?

As for the neo-Gaullists, whether from the right or the left, they maintain that nuclear weapons or the decision to use them cannot be shared. They cite reasons linked to sovereignty and the political situation of West Germany barred from acquiring nuclear weapons by the superpowers. They also raise questions about politico-strategic credibility. If the enemy harbors doubts about our use of strategic weapons to protect our own vital interests, then how much more doubtful would he be regarding Berlin or Hamburg?

The possibilities of cooperation on nuclear matters are limited. They exist in the civilian domain where, for example, the nuclear breeder-reactor Super-Phenix has European financial backing. But the basic decisions (placement, control, guarantee) cannot conceivably be shared. This is not because the French are unwilling to cooperate, but rather because nuclear logic limits considerably sharing sovereignty, whoever the partners may be.

Some will point out that there exists a nuclear planning group within NATO, and that it is therefore hard to see why France could not accept similar arrangements. Indeed, the idea of a defense council put forth by President Mitterrand after that of bilateral consultations, heads in that direction. But we must look lucidly at the *times* being discussed. These are consultations in *peacetime* to limit destruction in *wartime*. To be sure, the French can talk with the Germans about firing zones, just as they can discuss "target-sharing" with the British. However, studies of decisionmaking have shown that between SACEUR's request and the final decision in the chain of command, there was a lag of ten to thirteen hours. Even if the lags were shorter in wartime, joint decisionmaking would remain either a lie or a naive belief. Discussions of the use of nuclear weapons removes all meaning from the French deterrent whose strong points reside essentially in the freedom of choice that it affords in time of *crisis*. What matters is crisis management, not the legalism of peacetime or the uncertainty of wartime. The primary concern of the French will be to maintain their freedom of action during that time. Thus, one wonders about the latent functions of an "American-Soviet Center for the Reduction of Nuclear Risks" built around the creation of a permanent mechanism designed to maintain control over the main events of a nuclear crisis.

Apart from these considerations, certain French politicians are propounding a nuclear barrage based on Hadès missiles on the Elbe or on neutron bombs. This does not acknowledge that West Germany is not asking for anything of the kind, that she fears more numerous targets on her territory, or that she keeps pointing to her solidarity with the East Germans faced with longer-range nuclear weapons. Thus, two attitudes coexist in France. Most politicians feel the need to make proposals, while practitioners and experts believe there are concrete limits to what can in fact be proposed.

Cooperation in conventional areas seems to hold more possibilities. Indeed, France and Germany have numerous existing agreements. Maneuvers could be increased (indeed, who protests the French Navy's full participation in NATO maneuvers in the Mediterranean?) and organized with fewer formal and awkward reservations from the French side if certain Germans were willing to change their "when will you rejoin NATO?" discourse. French overtures (like the FAR) increase even if technical problems (like air cover) remain. Those developments, more than symbolic proposals of bi- or multilateral brigades, will boost cooperation. But, do the French overtures in this area always receive the support of the West German leadership which is little inclined to question the current forms of integration within NATO?

A thorough assessment should also cover institutional, industrial, and diplomatic areas. A security strategy that does not take these elements into account will, despite any protestations of good will, be condemned to repeating formulas and slogans. The less the strategy corresponds to reality, the more affective and symbolic will be the repetition of these formulas and slogans.

In order to avoid falling into the traps of polite speeches devoid of concrete meaning, certains conditions must be met. First, the different levels of mutual fears and misunderstandings need to be dealt with, whether we are talking about security or other subjects. We cannot make any progress nor go beyond fears and stumbling blocks without understanding each other's collective images.

If "security" is the objective we seek, as heirs of a history rife with violence experienced on our own soil, then its realization will come not just from the reduction of arms, but from the alleviation of our fears. The mere reduction of oversized arsenals does not affect our everyday lives. These fears, just like the perception of threats, are held partly in common and partly individually.

Without any analysis of resulting strategies, it is useless to create a joint brigade or to decide on nuclear targets. West Germany should tell us what she wants, and therefore know it herself. We can laugh at the French strategic pretensions or at its small-great power fantasies. But at least, one can discern objectives there, even if they are not, or cannot be, achieved. In the "strategic" dialogue with West Germany, which must take place before concrete overtures can be made, the French do not know what the Germans want. Nor do they know what the Germans have to offer, without which there cannot be a viable agreement. As long as West Germany does not know either what she wants or what she is offering, the French are condemned to go from worry to indifference, or worse, to change their mind.

Notes

This chapter was translated by Nancy Gil and Philippe Le Prestre.

1. Population density in France averages $100/km^2$, but is only $30/km^2$ in half of the country. The French are thus poorly acquainted with the presence of military forces, and there are no major phenomena of lassitude or rejection.

2. The positive German balance of payments in relation to France was 9.3 billion DM in 1985 and 12.4 billion DM in 1986.

CHAPTER 5

British-French Nuclearization and European Denuclearization: Implications for U.S. Policy

EDWARD A. KOLODZIEJ

The treaty signed by the United States and the Soviet Union in December 1987 to eliminate intermediate- and shorter-range missiles has significant implications for European security. Ratifications of the treaty open the way for additional superpower accords on strategic offensive and defensive systems. As the superpower nuclear balance is codified at the global level and regionally in Europe, pressures will inevitably mount on the United Kingdom and France to include their nuclear forces into superpower negotiations.

The size and sophistication of Franco-British nuclear forces and the extensive nuclear modernization programs that both countries have scheduled for completion in the 1990s will make it difficult for either country to remain isolated from the arms control process now under way. Both governments risk growing friction with one or both of the superpowers. Both will also be increasingly subject to criticisms from other allies and domestic opponents who seek to reduce nuclear arsenals and western reliance on nuclear deterrence as the basis for western strategy. Such criticisms already exist and are particularly strong in Great Britain.

This chapter argues that British and French participation in superpower nuclear negotiations could have a positive impact on European security and peace. Progress will depend, however, on major revisions in the bargaining stances of the Western nuclear states. The United States will be obliged to enlarge the scope and aims of its arms control policies vis-à-vis the Soviet Union and the Warsaw Pact. Specifically, it will have to incorporate the conditions set by London and Paris, to be examined in detail in a later section, for their participation in superpower talks. Until now, the United

States has tended to insulate its nuclear arms control discussions with the Soviet Union from the specific concerns of its European allies. The limits of this approach are now evident in light of widespread concern and criticism that has been prompted by the treaty throughout Europe.

Conversely, the British and French governments will be required to reexamine their reluctance to define the specific circumstances under which the conditions that they have defined for participation will have been met. They, too, will be under pressure to enlarge their notions—as they already show signs of doing—of their responsibilities for European security in light of growing superpower arms control accords and in response to powerful forces at work in Europe, largely arising from domestic sources, to redefine the bases for European security and alliance nuclear and non-nuclear strategy.

The first part of this chapter outlines the principal strategic problems posed by British and French nuclear forces for Western strategy and the East-West balance and discusses the conditions defined by Britain and France for their participation in superpower nuclear arms discussions.

The subsequent parts sketch the initiatives that need to be taken by the United States, Britain, and France if a new security regime for Europe is to enjoy long-term allied governmental and popular support and to serve the interests and aims of alliance members. These initiatives need to be taken at four closely related but distinct levels of government action that are essentially implied, as this analysis argues, by the conditions established by Britain and France for their entry into superpower arms talks. The incorporation of these conditions into the bargaining postures of the Western nuclear powers could have four useful outcomes, achievable in sequential but overlapping order: (1) a more stable superpower balance; (2) a more reliable Western nuclear deterrent; (3) a gradual shift from dependence on nuclear to conventional deterrence by both blocs, accompanied by cuts in conventional forces; and (4) as the nuclear and non-nuclear environments are stabilized, an East-West conflict oriented increasingly toward socioeconomic and political competition.

Problems Posed by British and French Nuclear Forces

France and Britain have the capability to destabilize superpower control when it may be most needed in a crisis; to prompt or to escalate conflict; to elicit, however unwittingly, preemptive strikes against British, French, and NATO forces; and to increase the chances of accidental, inadvertent, or unintentional nuclear war. Even where deliberation and calculation are present, both European nuclear powers may impose their preferred strategies, based on smaller military capabilities and a significantly narrower geographical base of operations, on the superpowers, potentially hastening a superpower nuclear exchange and resulting in widespread material damage and civilian loss of life.

The expansion and modernization of Franco-British forces also significantly complicate superpower arms control talks. Neither power currently participates in strategic arms reduction negotiations, and there is no formula on the negotiating table at Geneva to integrate their arsenals into the superpower balance. The Soviet Union confronts three Western nuclear forces (and a fourth with China). No Soviet planner can be indifferent to them.

The United States also faces tough choices at two distinct levels. As a superpower nuclear weapons accord progresses, it may have to choose between alliance cohesion and Soviet demands for compensation or control over Western nuclear systems, an issue already posed in negotiations over SALT (e.g., the transfer of cruise missile technology) and over the INF treaty (e.g., Bonn's possession of 72 Pershing IAs armed by the United States). And even if arms control progress is halted, the United States still has an interest in influencing the military strategies, deterrent moves, and targeting priorities governing British and French nuclear forces, as well as their composition, readiness, and deployment.

Capabilities

By the end of the 1990s, British and French nuclear forces, already impressive, will be formidable. Each will have invulnerable, second-strike forces capable of placing the Soviet Union at risk. Each can already inflict damage on the Soviet Union outweighing any conceivable gain that might tempt a Soviet attack on their homelands. The British Trident will comprise four submarines, each with sixteen D-5 missiles. The D-5, with a range of over four thousand miles, is, in a unique arrangement, to be leased from the United States. It will very likely be mounted by a U.S.-designed bus which will deliver up to eight independently targeted warheads to be produced by Great Britain.[1] U.S. buses are of two types. The Mk5 can carry eight W88 475-kiloton warheads; the Mk4, currently used in Trident I, can deliver twelve to fourteen W76 100-kiloton warheads.[2] As a unilateral arms control measure, aimed partially at blunting the criticisms of domestic opponents, the British government of Prime Minister Margaret Thatcher has announced that it will restrict planning to eight warheads, the maximum number of warheads carried by the C-4. Downplayed is the greater accuracy and throw-weight capacity of the D-5.[3] Britain's Trident could have as many as 512 warheads of approximately a half-megaton apiece.

For economic and strategic reasons, the Thatcher government may confine Trident to three full complements of missiles and warheads, i.e., about forty-eight missiles (plus spares) and 384 warheads, although there exists no confirmed evidence that British totals will be kept to these levels. These numbers are based on planning that foresees one submarine always on deep patrol; another preparing or in transit to relieve it; a third under service in port but potentially capable of firing in an emergency; and a fourth essentially out of commission and undergoing major refit and overhaul.[4]

If only one Trident submarine were available (two more likely in an emergency), Britain would still have awesome striking power to visit intolerable devastation on the Soviet Union. With four to five warheads aimed at each of the Soviet Union's twenty-two cities with a population of one million or more, all potentially within the range of the D-5, a single Trident submarine would conceivably threaten forty to forty-five million Soviets with the prompt effects of a nuclear explosion—and even more when radiation and widespread social dislocation in the wake of a nuclear attack are factored in.

French nuclear forces of the 1990s will be equally lethal. They will be built around six nuclear submarines. Each will carry sixteen French-built M-4 missiles, each MIRVed with six 150-kiloton warheads. Five of France's six nuclear submarines are undergoing refitting to replace their sixteen M-20 missiles, each with a one-megaton warhead, with the M-4 system. The sixth submarine will be replaced in the 1990s by a submarine of more advanced design. The M-4 will likely be replaced by an improved, more reliable M-5 missile. The French have three submarines always on station. If they build a full complement of missiles and warheads for their submarine forces, in contrast to likely British practice, they would have ninety-six missiles (plus spares) and at least 576 warheads. In addition, eighteen IRBMs, with a single megaton warhead, are stationed in southern France. Rounding out French strategic nuclear forces are eighteen aging Mirage IV bombers, with in-flight refueling capacity, which will be retained into the 1990s. These aircraft will be modernized with medium-range air-to-surface stand-off missiles (ASMPs) armed with a 100-to-300-kiloton warhead.[5] The first set of six of these modernized Mirage IVPs were deployed in May 1986.[6] Between them, France and Britain may have approximately one thousand strategic warheads at their disposal. Their submarine forces, once modernization is completed in the 1990s, will constitute about 20 percent of the West's sea-based deterrent.[7]

Strategy

Britain and France have pursued divergent strategies, aimed as much to influence U.S. as Soviet nuclear practice. While both have adopted in principle a policy of minimum deterrence, each has followed a contrasting approach in its efforts to influence the behavior of the superpowers: the British preferring officially to coordinate their forces and planning with those of the United States and NATO; the French, to distance themselves from Washington and to withdraw from NATO military cooperation within the Atlantic alliance to maximize their independence and, by that token, their leverage over U.S. and Soviet moves.

As a consequence of an agreement signed at a meeting in the Bahamas between Prime Minister Harold Macmillan and President John F. Kennedy, British Polaris forces, since December 1962, have been "assigned as a part of a NATO nuclear force and targeted in accordance with NATO plans."[8] This same understanding was carried forward under the agreement with the Carter and Reagan administrations to supply "Trident II missiles, equipment and supporting services on a continuing basis and in a manner generally similar to that in which Polaris was supplied."[9] If this understanding is read in isolation, it would appear that British nuclear forces are an integral part of NATO defenses; since the NATO commander is an American, British nuclear striking power would also seem to be under U.S. presidential control. Reinforcing this impression is the participation of British officers in target planning in developing the Single Integrated Operational Plan (SIOP) of the United States. Less assuring is the caveat, inserted by Prime Minister Macmillan in the Bahamas communiqué and repeated thereafter by succeeding British governments, that British forces might *not* be available "where Her Majesty's Government may decide that supreme national interests are at stake."[10]

Since 1962, the accent has shifted toward the independence of British nuclear forces in U.S. and British announced policies. Secretary of Defense Robert McNamara's reservations were overruled at the Bahamas meeting. In a speech in the spring of 1962, presumably with White House approval, he attacked independent

European nuclear systems as "dangerous, expensive, prone to obsolescence and lacking in credibility as a deterrent."[11] McNamara was never able to do much about blocking either the British or French system. As for Great Britain, Prime Minister Harold Macmillan, reportedly relying heavily on his personal rapport with President Kennedy, gained his consent to replace the canceled Skybolt air-to-surface missile, with Polaris missiles. This decision spelled the demise of Britain's V-Bomber force which needed Skybolt to penetrate continually improving Soviet air defenses.[12] With the demise of the U.S.-backed multilateral nuclear force in the mid-1960s, substantially undermined by British countermoves,[13] the British deterrent was freed of what remaining U.S. or NATO coil might have constrained it. In 1974, NATO ministers, meeting in Ottawa, affirmed the purported contribution of independent European nuclear systems, i.e., British and French forces, to Western deterrence.[14]

British leaders, while repeatedly acknowledging the integration of Britain's forces into NATO, underline the independence of its nuclear striking power. British missiles are said to add "a second center of decisionmaking" within the alliance and thereby reinforce deterrence against possible Soviet aggression. George Younger, Secretary of State for Defence, explained how decentralized alliance nuclear decisionmaking might work to deter a Soviet attack: "We have no doubt that [the U.S. nuclear] commitment remains as firm as ever. But in certain circumstances, the Soviet leadership might misjudge American resolve and miscalculate the consequences of aggression against western Europe. In such circumstances, British nuclear weapons would greatly complicate the calculations of Soviet leaders. They could not attack Europe without risking a strategic nuclear response."[15] Left unstated was the implication that Britain might have to act independently, either alone (if indeed the United States was not forthcoming) or to prompt a supportive U.S. initiative.

Emphasizing Britain's independent deterrent has made good domestic politics for the Thatcher government and, ironically, reinforced its standing in Washington. The Labour party apparently lost votes among some of its traditional supporters as well as some undecided voters for its insistence on Britain's unilateral renunciation of nuclear weapons.[16] The Reagan administration also viewed a Labour victory with concern lest Britain's denuclearization encourage neutralist sentiment in NATO. There was also the fear, widely held in policy circles and adroitly turned to advantage by the Thatcher government, that failure to renew the special nuclear relationship would lead to a cut in British conventional forces committed to NATO, a concern signaled by both Presidents Carter and Reagan in agreeing to U.S. help.[17]

Labour's nuclear position negated much of the credibility that the Reagan administration might have attached to its election proposal to reallocate funds from Trident to bolster British conventional forces, especially in Germany. In a reversal of mutual alliance expectations, Thatcher's Conservative party earned favor in Washington by insisting on Trident even at the cost of spending on non-nuclear arms while Labour lost Washington's confidence by pledging a larger British contribution to NATO's conventional readiness—what the Americans were on record as wanting—but at the expense of an independent nuclear deterrent. Many U.S. critics also doubted that Labour, once in office, would be able to deliver on its promise to strengthen Britain's conventional forces in the face of constituent pressures to increase welfare spending. Labour's campaign promise to negotiate the end of U.S. storage of nuclear weapons in the United Kingdom during the five-year lifetime of a parliament, if it should win election, reinforced U.S. skepticism about Labour's reliability as an ally.

As a quid pro quo for Trident, the Thatcher government will let U.S. nuclear-armed forces stay, but British forces can be expected to remain under tight national direction, while formally assigned to NATO. Whether they will be available when they are most needed as a deterrent or whether they will be subject to U.S. control in a confrontation with Moscow remains problematic. Meanwhile, the costs of the Trident system, in excess of ten billion pounds, are hampering fulfillment of Britain's promise to "upgrade its conventional forces," a key part of the rationale to sell Trident to the United Kingdom.[18] Spending on the British Army on the Rhine has already stagnated. Despite rising costs, expenditures have remained constant since 1985, and the Thatcher government has announced decreases in defense spending over three years that may approach 7 percent.[19]

U.S. influence over French nuclear forces appears much more tenuous. There is no special relationship between Washington and Paris to restrain France; French domestic opinion, unlike Britain's, heavily favors an independent nuclear force narrowing the potential impact of external pressures on public sentiment; and French nuclear capabilities are almost entirely indigenous (U.S.-supplied KC-135 tankers refuel Mirage bombers). Until the NATO Ottawa declaration, U.S.-French nuclear relations were as marked by controversy as those between Paris and Moscow.[20] French doctrine is unambiguous about total national control of nuclear forces in the hands of the French president.[21] French strategy is defined in terms of deterrence, and not of defense or of deterrence by denial.[22] France continues to refuse integration of its forces into NATO or into NATO's flexible response strategy. Conventional and tactical nuclear forces are primarily assigned roles subordinate to French strategic forces. They are to be independently used to test adversary intentions before a full nuclear strike is launched. If a full-scale Warsaw pact attack is under way, these forces may well be used in cooperation with NATO forces to repel a Soviet or Eastern bloc assault, but there exists no agreed-upon plan—nor is one envisaged—to coordinate French and NATO forces. The French president will use these forces at times and places of his choosing.

The NATO commander has no way of knowing when and if French conventional forces or facilities will be available, the contingencies under which French tactical nuclear forces might be used to test an attacker's determination, or the circumstances under which a strategic strike might be launched. From a Soviet perspective, it will be all but impossible to discriminate between a NATO or a French nuclear strike. Once hostilities begin, operational plans linking French and NATO forces are not in place to control the scope and extent of damage or to bring the conflict to a halt. Creating these uncertainties is precisely a major aim of French thinking, designed to influence both allied (specifically U.S.) and adversary behavior in ways deemed favorable by the French president.

The rigid separation of French and NATO forces dictated by de Gaulle and institutionalized in France's withdrawal from the NATO organization has gradually eroded as successive French presidents and governments have had to adjust to new strategic problems occasioned by the geographic constraints of the European battlefield, the modernization of superpower offensive and defensive systems as well as shifts in their balance, and the evolution of arms control negotiations.[23] Since the mid-1970s, French planners have accepted the notion of a single European battlefield, rejecting earlier, artificial distinctions between a battle for Western Europe and for the national sanctuary. The Socialist government created a Rapid Action Force (*Force d'Action Rapide*, FAR) in the 1980s, composed of helicopter gunships and quickly deployable forces to reinforce France's approximately fifty thousand troops stationed in Germany. The FAR implements the single battle idea by providing the French president with an option to engage French forces early in the battle for Europe or to deploy them in forward positions in a crisis to underscore French resolve. Paris was also one of the staunchest supporters of U.S. INF deployments to ensure a common allied stance against the Soviet Union and to anchor West Germany to the Western alliance.

France's nuclear modernization program also partly responds to allied concerns. The Hadès, a ground-based tactical nuclear system (with a range of 450 km), will replace Pluton, whose short-range (125 km) made it more a threat to West Germany than to Eastern bloc forces. Even under the de Gaulle regime, France promoted joint weapons programs and entered into more bilateral arrangements than any other European state.[24] Since the 1970s France has also been increasingly responsive to U.S. nonproliferation concerns, resisting Iraqi, Pakistani, and South Korean requests for expanded nuclear cooperation. At U.S. urging, it sent troops to Lebanon. If it refused overflight rights to U.S. F-111s based in Britain against the Khadafi regime in 1986, it did coordinate its substantial efforts in Chad with those of the United States to assist the defeat of more heavily armed Libyan forces by those of Hissène Habré. All these moves, however, still do not add up to an integrated French-NATO approach to nuclear deterrence, nor is there any political sentiment among any of France's major parties to even reexamine de Gaulle's decision to withdraw from NATO.

Targeting

British and French targeting plans emphasize penetration of Soviet defenses to deliver unacceptable damage on the Soviet Union, relying exclusively on nationally controlled nuclear forces. Until recently, British planners have been attached to the so-called Moscow criterion. British planners have long felt that the test of a credible British deterrent was its ability to threaten Moscow since it is the seat of the Soviet government and purportedly of such high value in Soviet eyes that it is the site of the only antimissile system permitted by the ABM treaty. The British modernized the warhead system carried by their Polaris fleet with the Chevaline in the 1970s to overwhelm Moscow's Golash antimissile system.[25] The Chevaline is a multiple, but not a MIRVed or independently targeted, reentry vehicle. Warheads impact on a defined target in close proximity of each other, leaving a larger footprint than the earlier one-megaton warhead of the Polaris A3. The capacity of the Chevaline bus, while secret, is reportedly composed of up to three 200-kiloton warheads with decoys and penetration aids.

The Trident II system of D-5 missiles and MIRVed warheads has expanded the British notion of the material requirements of minimum deterrence, while creating new options for Britain's target menu. In justifying the decision to buy Trident I in 1980 (later upgraded in 1982 by the purchase of the more capable D-5 or Trident II missile), the Thatcher government went well beyond the Moscow criterion in characterizing its targeting approach to the Soviet Union:

> The Government does not believe that our deterrent arm would be adequately met by a capability which offered only a low likelihood of striking home to key targets; or which posed the prospect of only a very small number of strikes; or which Soviet leaders could expect to ward off successfully from large areas of key importance to them. . . . The Government . . . thinks it right now to make clear that their concept of deterrence is concerned essentially with posing a potential threat to key aspects of Soviet state power.[26]

It is difficult to reconcile NATO's flexible response strategy under U.S. presidential control through the NATO commander with Britain's targeting plans to threaten "key aspects of Soviet power." To be credible, the British deterrent would have to be able to act independently to convince Soviet planners to desist from some proscribed behavior adverse to British interests. Soviet leaders would have to be convinced, as a British White Paper observed, that Britain would launch an attack "if they [the Soviets] thought at some critical point as a conflict developed the US would hold back."[27] But British nuclear forces would also have to be able to act if the United States *did* hold back. As targets expand to the warheads available, the wider targeting menu available to British planners may tempt earlier use of nuclear weapons than the Moscow criterion as targeters seek to define intermediary steps between an ineffective conventional response and all-out nuclear war in the face of a Warsaw Pact attack. Even if one were not to assume so pessimistic a scenario—highly improbable since the very existence of Britain as a nation would be risked—British nuclear planners are being led to think in war-fighting and damage-limit terms simply because they have more warheads at their disposal.

Unlike Britain, France is unambiguous about the need for autonomous control of national nuclear forces and targeting plans in the face of whatever pressures or provocations might be initiated by either or both superpowers.[28] Since de Gaulle's rejection of the Kennedy administration's proposal for a NATO multilateral nuclear force, initially a part of the Polaris offer to Britain, the French have successfully resisted any U.S. attempt to exercise influence over the size, composition, or employment of their nuclear forces. French strategy also seeks to minimize the risk of being drawn into a nuclear war against its wishes through too close French association with the United States. France's refusal to allow U.S. use of French airspace in launching an attack on Libya in April 1986 with British-based F-111 bombers illustrates French reluctance to cooperate with the United States in joint military operations.

French targeting plans appear to be evolving in a way similar to Britain's. As capabilities have grown, so also has France's thinking about its targeting menu expanded and its notion of what is required for minimum deterrence. The French have adopted an "enlarged anticity" posture, apparently including in their target list important economic, administrative, and political sites as well as cities and industrial centers. This expanded list of targets suggests more a French objective of increasing the scope and probability of damage to the Soviet Union than the adoption of a war-fighting strategy. For France and Britain, the latter course is beyond their resources and geopolitically ruled out given the disparities between them and the Soviet Union.

In striking what some French writers call the "vital works" of an adversary—*oeuvres vives*[29]—more human and material destruction may be wrought than concentrating solely on Soviet cities, since the devastation would be greater in scope and more lasting. There is some basis for believing that the destruction of a nation's civilian support infrastructure may have more devastating effect in the long run than simply attacking military targets or population centers. A recent MIT computer simulation of alternative targeting plans suggests that attacking the energy-producing infrastructure of the Soviet Union would have a greater retarding effect upon long-term recovery efforts than targeting associated simply with destroying cities.[30]

In contrast to Britain, France is significantly enlarging its nonstrategic nuclear forces as integral parts of its preplanned deterrent moves. These nuclear elements, comprising independently armed air, sea, and ground units, have been designated pre-strategic forces. Again, there are no plans, in contrast to British Tornado aircraft or ships, currently armed, respectively, with British-made free-falling bombs and depth charges, to coordinate the employment of France's pre-strategic forces with NATO responses. These nuclear forces are ostensibly designed to test Soviet-bloc aims in an attack and to signal French escalatory intentions by inflicting significant military damage on enemy forces. Speaking of the nuclear message to be carried by Hadès (or presumably other French pre-strategic forces), French Armed Forces Chief of Staff Jeannou Lacaze insisted that it "have military effect, which is to say that it must be effective and brutal, which means a relatively massive employment and therefore limited in time and space. But above all this warning must be integrated in the general deterrent maneuver."[31]

Anglo-French Conditions to Arms Control Participation

Neither London nor Paris is interested in participating in superpower nuclear arms limitation talks before their modernization programs are completed. Both successfully weathered Soviet pressures to be counted in negotiations over long-range ballistic systems in Europe. Both contended that their national systems were strategic, not theater; neither, moreover, is ultimately subject to NATO or U.S. control. Moscow acceded to this position in proposing its breakthroughs on intermediate- and shorter-range missiles. The Soviet Union appears less flexible on national strategic systems. It has already served notice through Chief of Staff Marshall Sergei Akhromeyev that British and French forces would have to enter "the global armaments process" at some point in the wake of a European missile accord.[32]

Britain and France have set stiff conditions to their consideration of being drawn into superpower offensive and defensive strategic arms limitation talks. First, there would have to be substantial decreases in U.S. and Soviet offensive striking power. Neither European nuclear power defines what "substantial" is. Even a reduction of 50 percent to six thousand warheads, as have been proposed at Geneva, might not meet Anglo-French demands. Fifty percent cuts would still leave superpower totals at a level over ten times greater than either European nuclear power. While Prime Minister Margaret Thatcher has not ruled out British participation, the chances of inducing her government into talks would appear to be slight if left entirely to a bean-counting exercise: "If between the two powers, the numbers went down massively and enormously and we moved into an entirely different world . . . then there may be circumstances when ours [British nuclear forces] will have to be counted."[33] Not only the nuclear beans in the jar will have to diminish but the jar itself—"an entirely different world"—will presumably have to be safe and shock-resistant before London will submit its forces to negotiation. France has entered a similar condition. The five-year defense planning document of the Chirac government presented to the National Assembly in 1986 affirmed that "the verifiable reduction of the nuclear arsenals of the United States and the Soviet Union constitutes the first step of a general process of nuclear disarmament."[34] Whether France will enter into nuclear arms control negotiations will depend on reductions in Soviet and U.S. arsenals to a point "where the disparity which exists between them and other nuclear powers will have changed *in nature.*"[35]

Second, both European powers insist on no fundamental changes in superpower development of defensive nuclear systems, including ABM, ASW, and passive measures. This is a critical consideration for both European nuclear powers. Unless their forces can survive a first strike and still penetrate alerted Soviet defenses, the credibility of their deterrent forces is placed in serious question. The British Chevaline was specifically designed to penetrate Soviet ABM defenses; the D-5 is in turn a "hedge against a breakdown of the ABM treaty regime and possible new deployments by the Soviets."[36]

The French also feel that they have most to lose by progress in superpower antimissile development. In a presentation to the National Assembly, former Socialist Defense Minister Charles Hernu argued that superpower competition in developing defense systems against nuclear attack would prompt an arms race, dismantle the space and ABM treaties, sanctuarize the homelands of the two superpowers at the expense of U.S. alliance commitments and extended deterrence, and accentuate the conventional imbalance in Europe in the Eastern bloc's favor.[37] André Giraud, Minister of Defense in the Chirac government, was less pointed than his predecessor, but shared the latter's serious reserve about the system: "SDI, for an indefinite period, will remain a factor of destabilization. It reinforces neither the security of France nor that of Europe."[38]

Third, France has explicitly entered a third condition, viz., significant reductions to end the "disequilibrium" in Europe favoring the Warsaw Pact conventional arms and the elimination of the threat of chemical weapons.[39] Britain's reaction to Soviet proposals to cut missiles in Europe also evidences a sensitivity to perceived Eastern bloc superiority in non-nuclear armaments. While opinion differs whether London has explicitly defined this as a condition, it has on more than one occasion underlined the importance of "eliminating conventional disparities" in Europe that currently disadvantage the West.[40] A superpower strategic arms agreement that was not linked in principle to conventional reductions by Soviet bloc forces would receive a cool reception in both European capitals.

Inducing either Britain or France to the negotiating table will not be easy. The conditions they have defined for participation are so general that even follow-on superpower accords on offensive and defensive strategic systems may not satisfy either European nuclear power. The French are especially resistant to superpower overtures. The domestic consensus favoring a French nuclear deterrent is strong across all political parties, however much they may differ over other defense priorities, particularly the role of tactical or pre-strategic forces. Even with deep cuts, superpower offensive totals might still be considered insufficient to constitute a change "in nature" when related to French and British totals. The French still prefer to increase their own nuclear forces rather than rely on international arms control accords for their security. The superpower treaty to eliminate intermediate- and shorter-range systems is still widely criticized in governmental circles,[41] and enjoyed more the acquiescent than the enthusiastic approval of the Chirac government.[42] If substantial asymmetrical cuts must also be made in conventional and chemical arms by the Soviet bloc before France will enter into arms control talks, it is difficult to see when that might occur. One is almost tempted to conclude that the conditions for French participation will not be fulfilled short of the completion of its nuclear modernization program.

The British have assumed a more supple position. The domestic consensus is fundamentally split on a national nuclear deterrent. The British have never said "never." Sir Geoffrey Howe, secretary of state for Foreign and Commonwealth Affairs, outlined the British position in what has become an often cited speech before the UN General Assembly in September 1983:

> As far as the British deterrent is concerned, we must naturally take into account that our force is a strategic one, and that it represents less than 3% of the strategic nuclear forces available to the United States or the Soviet Union. It would be absurd as things stand for us to seek to trade reductions with a super power. But we have never said 'never.' On the contrary, we have made it clear that, if Soviet and US strategic arsenals were to be very substantially reduced, and if no significant changes had occurred in Soviet defensive capabilities, Britain would want to review her position and to consider how best she could contribute to arms control in the light of the reduced threat. That remains our position.[43]

The United States is in a delicate position. If it pressures its allies to cut their arsenals, it risks splitting the alliance and weakening the credibility of its nuclear guaranty to Europe. If it ignores the problems posed by independent nuclear forces and allows the European systems to be primarily defined by the national economic and technological resources devoted to them, progress on arms control with the Soviet Union may be seriously impeded and even arrested. If the United States compensates the Soviet Union too generously for British and French nuclear forces over which it has little or no direct control, it may create the worst of all worlds: heightening allied perception of U.S. willingness to lower its commitment to European defense; increasing pressures on Britain and France to expand their nuclear forces at the expense of conventional capabilities; and isolating Germany even more as its principal allies adopt increasingly unilateralist positions, insensitive to the domestic pressures on Bonn to agree to enter into negotiations for the denuclearization of all bloc forces stationed in Central Europe. The neutralist drift in German domestic policy would be strengthened as would the sentiment that German security interests depended more on accommodating Soviet wishes than on tending to crumbling Western defenses.

Turning a Problem into an Opportunity: Breaking the Impasse

The responsibility for breaking the impasse over British and French participation in strategic arms talks lies, nevertheless, more with Washington than with Moscow—or even with the European states. Neither Britain nor France can be expected to limit its nuclear modernization program or to accept restraints on their operational use unless both countries are assured about the reliability of the nuclear deterrent regime for Europe, including the U.S. guaranty, on terms responsive to their differing strategic needs and acceptable to the differentiated constraints posed by their domestic politics and public opinion. To prepare the path to participation, the United States can take a number of steps that would relax British and French reservations. First it will have to listen before it will be heard.

Both Britain and France want a superpower-negotiated security regime for Europe that strengthens deterrence against the Soviet Union but promotes peaceful political and economic exchange and engagement. The contradictory stances assumed by the United States on nuclear policy over the past decade have repeatedly challenged British and French preference for a policy of deterrence cum détente. On the one hand, U. S. abandonment of the SALT process, the gradual erosion of SALT II limits, and aggressive implementation of the Strategic Defense Initiative (SDI) in the 1980s signaled what appeared to be a unilateralist bent in U.S. nuclear strategy and a disconcerting U.S. commitment to a war-fighting strategy driven by the aim of nuclear superiority. While London and Paris initially welcomed an expansion and modernization of the U.S. nuclear arsenal as well as INF deployments to match Soviet strategic and theater forces, the latter as much a symbolic political gesture as a response to strategic requirements, both supported observance of SALT I and II limits and continued superpower negotiations on arms reductions. Neither wanted an unregulated arms race that would threaten its own nuclear forces; heighten East-West tensions and arrest détente in Europe; increase pressures on already tight national defense budgets, galvanizing domestic opponents against increased defense expenditures (particularly troublesome in Britain); strain alliance cohesion over burden sharing and over priorities to be assigned nuclear and non-nuclear forces or, specifically, upset the French security consensus forced to confront hard decisions for new spending from a narrow resource base.

On the other hand, the Reykjavik summit, where President Reagan proposed eliminating all ballistic missiles in ten years, and Washington's quick and what many in Europe viewed as expedient embrace of Premier Gorbachev's double-zero option for intermediate- and shorter-range missiles raised fears in London and Paris that the United States might weaken its nuclear commitment to Europe and give impetus to its denuclearization for the sake of an arms accord with the Soviet Union. British Prime Minister Margaret Thatcher's November 1986 visit to Washington, in the wake of the Reykjavik meeting, was hastily undertaken precisely to limit the damage of the president's proposals. Thatcher elicited the president's pledge—so-called Camp David II—to discipline U.S. arms control to the needs of European deterrence and to restrict the U.S. negotiating position at Geneva to 50 percent cuts in superpower warhead inventories.[44] Damage to the prestige of the Reagan administration over Iran-*contra* disclosures has simply lent urgency to European concerns about U.S. resolve as well as its capacity to lead, hence Prime Minister Margaret Thatcher's hasty trip in July 1987 to lend support to the Reagan administration beleaguered by the controversy with Congress.

Superpower conflict or condominium, reflecting wild swings in U.S. policy pronouncements and behavior, have become real, if alternating, possibilities. The three conditions defined by Britain and France for their participation in strategic arms talks are essentially hedges against either unsought contingency. Only if the United States incorporates these conditions into its negotiating position toward the Soviet Union, while containing the temptation to act unilaterally, can they be induced to pay lower premiums on their nuclear insurance policies to protect their interests and to cooperate in building a more stable European security regime.

Negotiating a Stabler Nuclear Environment

First, the United States should negotiate a nuclear environment with the Soviet Union unambiguously dedicated to stable deterrence, not superiority. SDI is a touchstone of U.S. intentions. It remains the major source of concern for NATO allies and the Soviet Union. According to British Foreign Secretary Geoffrey Howe, who summarized the European critique in 1985, SDI fosters a mutually supportive offensive-defensive arms race, undermines the strategic arms control process by eroding the ABM treaty, and damages deterrence by decoupling U.S. and European security interests; and it does all this for no purpose since ABM defenses can be easily overwhelmed by readily available countermeasures.[45] Howe's criticism, as sharp and probing as any emanating from Moscow, came in the wake of Prime Minister Margaret Thatcher's failure to gain President Reagan's adherence in practice to the Anglo-American understanding of December 1984. The communiqué emerging from Camp David I, recognized more in the breach by the Reagan administration than in the observance, pledged both parties to four aims:

1. The U.S. and Western aim is not to achieve superiority but to maintain balance, taking into account Soviet developments.
2. SDI-related deployment would, in view of treaty obligations, have to be a matter of negotiations.
3. The overall aim is to enhance, not undercut, deterrence.
4. East-West negotiations should aim to achieve security with reduced levels of offensive systems on both sides.[46]

Two years later, British concerns about the U.S. SDI program had not been stilled. In an address to the International Institute for Strategic Studies, Howe again referred to his 1985 reservations about SDI, adding that "we have to accept that not everything technically possible may be affordable or prudent."[47] Adapting SDI to a stable deterrent regime would quiet allied misgivings and foster progress in superpower strategic talks.

London and Paris have pursued contrasting routes to diminish the adverse impact of SDI on their nuclear forces and, specifically, on the multilateral deterrence regime on which their security interests depend. Following traditional practice, the British have tried to limit SDI by influencing U.S. policy from within. They were the first to sign a memorandum of understanding with the Pentagon to help British firms compete for SDI contracts. Prime Minister

Thatcher has also personally tried to find a compromise between the U.S. and Soviet position by introducing the notion of "feasibility" in component testing.[48] A wider range of research and development would be permitted under Thatcher's formula than under the Soviet position, but one narrower than the Reagan administration's preferred interpretation that would essentially reject all treaty restraints on research, testing, and development. France, where skepticism about SDI unites political parties, has been more direct in its criticism of SDI. It has also launched an alternative to SDI in the Eureka program under European Community auspices to encourage European civilian high-tech cooperation. While the Chirac government encouraged national firms to compete for SDI contracts (why not eavesdrop on the U.S. SDI program while winning lucrative and technologically beneficial contracts), France has not signed a formal agreement with the United States to guide and facilitate bilateral cooperation.[49]

SDI and its Soviet counterpart, even more than the multiplication of superpower offensive capabilities, threaten British and French nuclear forces. Neither has the resources to keep pace in an offensive-defensive superpower nuclear arms race. Both prefer to restrain Soviet (and U.S.) anti-ABM efforts by preserving as much of the ABM treaty as possible, using SDI as a bargaining chip to induce Soviet compromises on deep cuts in offensive forces and on defensive systems. Such an approach would also reconcile U.S. support of the British Trident program and the Ottawa declaration. There is a fundamental contradiction in proclaiming the value of independent nuclear deterrent forces in NATO, at no small cost to the states involved, while working to undermine their effectiveness.

To create incentives for British-French participation in superpower talks, SDI need only be brought into line with its limits: growing budgetary restraints occasioned by mounting U.S. deficits, declining congressional support, Soviet-allied objections and, not least of all, preponderant scientific opinion about SDI's modest prospects.[50] A step forward would be to stand still, the putative aim of the congressional restriction, sponsored by Senator Sam Nunn, to preclude SDI deployments for a year. Meanwhile, negotiations at Geneva can focus on acceptable research and development within the terms of the treaty and on verification measures to preclude cheating or breakout. Not only would the arms talks be advanced, but U.S. policy would be harmonized with the broad aims of the December 1984 Thatcher-Reagan communiqué. A principal (but by no means the only) stumbling block to a superpower accord on strategic weapons will have been eliminated. The United States will then have returned unequivocally to the principle of a negotiated, not unilaterally imposed, nuclear environment in which British and French forces can be reasonably expected to contribute in stabilizing, not disrupting, its European component.

A More Reliable and Stable Western Nuclear Deterrent

Second, the United States should use its leverage to elicit British and French cooperation in constructing a more reliable and stable Western deterrent as an integral part of the evolving superpower regime. The United States, as the strongest member of the Western alliance and still Europe's guarantor, is the strategic bridge between the four nuclear systems. (It built one, balances another, sustains a third, and has at different times sold equipment and know-how to bolster a fourth.) It is in the most favorable position to lead in negotiating a multilateral deterrent regime for Europe that responds not only to its own needs and interests but to the competing requirements of its allies and principal adversary.

Possible Areas of Atlantic Cooperation

There are several ways to give impetus and direction to an expanded Western and Soviet-American arms control process. As a start, the Anglo-American special relationship should be gradually extended to France. The pace of this process would necessarily have to be pragmatically calibrated to the technical and military opportunities for expansion arising from mutually perceived strategic needs (e.g., exchange of intelligence or technology) and to the relaxation of domestic constraints on cooperation (strong in France but not negligible in the United States and Britain).

At a minimum, the French may well be disposed to U.S. proposals to reduce accidental, unintended, unauthorized, or preemptive use of French and British nuclear forces while reinforcing their invulnerability and penetrability. France's submarine force has several problems. Its submarines reportedly run louder, slower, travel closer to the surface and have less range, station time, and durability than the U.S. or British Trident. The reliability and efficiency of their C3I systems also need to be improved, evidenced by continuing high-level transatlantic talks between officials and experts on French and NATO C3I systems. Improvements in these categories could be achieved through Anglo-American technology transfers. Such exchanges would be especially appealing in the construction of the seventh and future submarines that will undoubtedly be authorized to replace France's aging fleet. Data about acoustical and nonacoustical ASW research and development, and even joint work in these fields, would keep the French force abreast of latest Western efforts and, through intelligence transfers, of Soviet progress. Other possible areas for greater cooperation, where France is dependent on its allies, are early warning of attack and target acquisition and evaluations.[51]

Penetration and assured destruction are functions of timely warning, responsive C3I systems under tight political control, and accurate targeting and guidance data and systems. On all these scores France needs assistance. The recent high priority assigned to the development of a reconnaissance satellite in the French defense budget in the next five-year plan underscores French concerns about the blind spots in the *force de frappe*'s space support system. The military satellite systems available to the superpowers, as one knowledgeable observer concludes, "are beyond France's national capability and can only be realized on a European scale."[52] There is some evidence that the French have instituted their own permissive action links (PAL) to ensure positive political control over its nuclear weapons.[53] Whether they are adequate would be an obvious topic for Franco- and Anglo-American exchanges. A Western hotline would also improve procedures for crisis management. The nine joint working groups covering U.S. and British collaboration and data exchange on Trident could be enlarged on an ad hoc basis to draw French and Anglo-American planning into closer alignment over time without fundamentally constraining independent national use.[54]

In return for U.S. assistance, the British and French contribution to European nuclear stability might assume several forms. Increased communication among the Western powers, tighter operational and political control of nuclear weapons, and discussions on targeting and crisis management procedures could strengthen Western arms control practices and protocols. Caps would also be placed on British and French nuclear modernization as compensation for U.S. aid for superpower concessions to limit their offensive and defensive nuclear systems.

Limits on Franco-British forces, as a bargaining lever to induce superpower cuts, might apply to the number of submarines, missiles, warheads, and throw weight—or to some combination of these elements to achieve overall reductions in the strategic systems of the Soviet Union and the Western nuclear powers. For example, the British and French might be held to four and five submarines, respectively. The British might be restricted to thirty missiles plus spares to arm three of their four submarines with ten missiles. Each loaded submarine would carry eighty (10 X 8) warheads. Four of France's five submarines would be loaded with ten missiles, but each boat would have sixty warheads (10 X 6). Both countries would then have 240 warheads in their inventories. The British and French would be expected to have, respectively, at least two and three submarines on station in a crisis or 160 and 180 warheads at their disposal. The higher operational totals for the French would be offset by the higher expected throw weight and warhead accuracy of the British Trident system. Such a combined force on station or each alone would still be able to inflict intolerable damage on the Soviet Union.

Franco-British Incentives to Cooperate

It is difficult to anticipate how the two European systems might be composed since their configurations would be the product of inter-allied and superpower bargaining. The more important point is the need for the creation of Western tripartite negotiations to avoid surprises and disarray in negotiations with the Soviet Union. A smaller Trident force, framed by corresponding deep superpowers cuts in offensive forces, would potentially have appeal for the Thatcher government. It could ensure Britain's requirements for an independent nuclear deterrent for this century, promote a broader domestic consensus (based on a smaller Trident) to sustain the program over its lifetime, and enlist London's active participation in defining Europe's security regime for the next decade.

France poses a more difficult obstacle. The mutual suspicions and failed expectations characterizing French and Anglo-American security relations throughout most of this century will not be easily overcome. Despite a flawed historical record and still strongly lingering Gaullist strictures evidenced in former Prime Minister Jacques Chirac's remarks before high-level officials of the French security community in December 1987,[55] the growing debate within France over strategic policy suggests that a new generation of French leaders is acutely aware that, unless France assumes full occupancy of its arms control chair in response to a new international environ-ment fundamentally different from the one that confronted Presi-dent de Gaulle a generation ago, France faces the prospect that its security interests will be defined without its assistance—a kind of strategic Yalta. Several powerful factors that are changing the systemic context are forcing a major, if reluctant, reorientation of French thinking and policy, reflected, as suggested below, in renewed French interest in cooperation with its Atlantic and European allies.

First, U.S. flirtations with strategies to abandon deterrence, either by seeking a compelling nuclear superiority or by erecting impenetrable defenses against nuclear attack, reflect a chronic tendency in U.S. policy supported within the U.S. security community across political and partisan lines. From a European perspective, this inclination can be explained as an attempt to escape the dangers and frustrations of the superpower balance of terror, but is no less ominous for being reasonable if narrowly viewed through U.S. security lenses.

U.S. withdrawal symptoms from nuclear deterrence, whether through a vain search for military superiority or through political arrangements with the Soviet Union over the heads of the West Europeans, have appeared in earlier transformations. The Kennedy administration's brief adoption of a counterforce strategy in the early 1960s illustrates the superiority syndrome. Nuclear deterrence was equated with nuclear superiority, to bolster a diplomatic position capable of levering concessions from the Soviet Union on U.S. terms. Conversely, U.S. arms control strategies—the Partial Test Ban in the 1960s and the nonproliferation treaty (both aimed partially at France) and the Carter administration's management of SALT II and cancellation of the neutron bomb (a blow to the Schmidt government in Germany)—manifest a U.S. proclivity to override European perceptions of their security interests through explicit or implicit accord with the Soviet Union.[56] European doubts about the U.S. nuclear commitment were reinforced by the Reykjavik summit, where President Reagan repeatedly proposed eliminating all ballistic missiles in ten years and by Washington's swift and what many in Europe viewed as expedient embrace of Premier Gorbachev's double-zero option for missiles with ranges between 300 and 3000 miles.

Skepticism about U.S. nuclear policies is especially widespread in France. The report of the defense committee of the French National Assembly of November 1987 was particularly pointed in its criticism of U.S. arms control aims and motivation:

> American leaders have certainly tried to reassure Europeans. In an article published in *Le Monde* on September 10 [1987], the American Secretary of Defense, Caspar Weinberger . . . reaffirmed the indivisible character of security between the United States and Europe, emphasized the American nuclear forces still present in Europe—bombers and nuclear submarines assigned to NATO—and underlined the need to modernize the capacity of the Atlantic Alliance to respond with conventional means.
>
> One would like to be convinced. Several considerations unfortunately make the case uncertain:

(a) Graduated response is raised in question; . . .

(b) The American nuclear forces which remain in Europe are by and large aging; . . .

(c) The modernization of conventional forces does not constitute a very convincing response; . . .

(d) One will recall finally that the Strategic Defense Initiative (SDI) does not constitute . . . a response adapted to the situation of European states.[57]

The U.S. inclination to escape the risks of nuclear deterrence is endemic to the U.S.-European security relation. Containing these withdrawal tendencies, whether manifested in U.S. behavior by expanding offensive and defensive nuclear systems to superpower destabilizing levels or by reducing their presence and commitment to Europe, must now be considered a continuing imperative of European (and French) strategic policy. De Gaulle counted on the U.S. guaranty even while disparaging its credibility because he shrewdly calculated that it was in the interests of the United States to defend Europe. Less clear today is whether U.S. public opinion or leaders will define these interests in the same way as European or French leaders. As Pierre Hassner has observed, European concerns about the stability of deterrence in Europe "consist less in knowing what the protector will do in case of aggression, nor even what the aggressor believes the protector will do, than what the protected believe that the aggressor believes that the protector will do."[58]

Gaining those assurances from U.S. leaders, increasingly bent by economic problems or internal demands for more burden sharing by Europeans, will not be easy. Meanwhile, the French are more convinced than ever, under the threat of additional U.S. withdrawals, that the American presence on the European continent, in the words of former Prime Minister Jacques Chirac, is "an absolute necessity."[59] France will be obliged to address U.S. demands for European cooperation as compensation for the U.S. guaranty. Concessions on both sides, as the discussion below suggests, could be mutually beneficial if they are cast in terms of a new security regime for Europe in which France could be expected to make an important contribution as part of a transatlantic bargain to retain U.S. support while promoting a relaxation of tensions with the Soviet Union.

A second change in France's strategic environment is West Germany's growing ambiguity, facing uneasily toward the East for détente and toward the West for security based on a strategy of nuclear deterrence which itself is increasingly disputed within Germany.[60] Undermined is the Gaullist expectation of Bonn's solid attachment to the Western security system. De Gaulle could have assumed U.S. protection as long as the Washington-Bonn connection held. West Germany was both the vehicle through which the U.S. strategic guaranty to continental Europe passed and the glacis behind which the French nuclear deterrent could maneuver. U.S. protection could be enlisted without the compensating burden of sharing risks and costs on the same basis as France's European allies that remained in NATO.[61]

Growing neutralist, pacifist, and anti-American sentiment within West Germany disposes the Bonn government to Soviet threats and blandishments.[62] In contrast to London and Paris, Bonn's *Ostpolitik* is formulated in terms of détente cum deterrence, whether the Christian or Social Democrats are in power. West Germany has the most to lose if the hard-won gains of détente are nullified and its development arrested. The Federal Republic's unrequited aspirations—increased and easier exchanges with East Germany and Eastern Europe, relaxed tensions with Moscow, and, over time, the gradual effacing if not the elimination of Germany's division—are more in Moscow's power to give than the West's to grant.

What most European governments currently fear, a rapid withdrawal of U.S. troops and a diminution of the U.S. nuclear guaranty, is actually welcomed by a vocal and increasing significant minority in Europe, particularly those in the Northern Tier. The opposition parties in Great Britain and West Germany favor progressive denuclearization of Europe. The British Labour party as well as the German Social Democratic and Green parties have broken with official NATO and U.S. strategy. They support a new security regime based on "defensive" forces by both camps. Placing reliance on the reform movement now under way in the Soviet Union, they are optimistic about Soviet willingness to cooperate in building a European security system from the Atlantic to the Urals. In such a scheme, the two blocs would be gradually dissolved and the role of the United States (whose nuclear policies are cited as a major threat to peace) would diminish. Sentiment in the Benelux and Scandinavian countries also runs high in favor of this reorientation.[63] Only French domestic policies appear to be largely insulated from these tendencies. However, it is doubtful whether France alone can withstand the pressures. It can either try to shape them, as President Mitterrand did in supporting INF deployments, or be shaped by them.

Third, the dynamism and flexibility of current Soviet arms diplomacy under the Gorbachev regime, alert to exploitable splits in alliance cohesion and in the domestic consensus of Western states on security, might well succeed where military threats previously failed to denuclearize Europe or to decrease the opportunities of Western resort to nuclear weapons or threats. This constitutes yet another challenge to French strategy and policies. There was always the dim possibility but not the imminent likelihood of a superpower arms accord that might progressively denuclearize Europe, isolating France's *force de frappe* and the British deterrent while subjecting the continental states, particularly West Germany, to Eastern bloc pressures arising from what many in Europe believe to be its preponderant non-nuclear forces. Moscow's aggressive campaign against nuclear weapons, publicly signaled in a major party document in January 1986,[64] and the success of Gorbachev's double-zero option and diplomacy of charm no longer rule out Europe's gradual denuclearization without counterbalancing reductions in the East's non-nuclear forces.

Fourth, emerging U.S. and German arms control stances, arising from shifting attitudes toward nuclear weapons and diverging national assessments of security interests, raise serious problems for the political and strategic viability of France's nuclear policies on which the current consensus on the *force de dissuasion* rests. On the one hand, rising sentiment within the Kohl government, led by Foreign Minister Hans-Dietrich Genscher, favors opening talks on the so-called third zero-option covering short-range nuclear missiles, most of which are based in Germany, rather than on conventional and chemical arms preferred by France and Britain. The latter approach is designed to forestall further weakening of nuclear deterrence as the basis of Europe's security. Public opinion in Germany, reflected in recent polls,[65] is also inclined toward nuclear disarmament and progress in ameliorating East-West relations by accommodating Soviet preferences. There is, moreover, the widespread feeling, even among German NATO supporters, that Germany is being asked to assume a disproportionate share of the alliance's nuclear risks—the so-called "singularization" issue. "The shorter the range of missiles," say Bonn officials privately, "the deader the Germans."

On the other hand, there is weakening support in the United States, as noted earlier, for current levels of U.S. conventional forces in Europe. Budgetary and trade deficits are producing constraints on spending while prompting increased congressional calls for reduction in military commitments and greater European burden-sharing. The global stock market crash in October 1987 and a faltering dollar invite demands for more cutbacks. Conversely, there is little indication that Europe and, specifically, Germany are prepared to fill the breach. Bonn resists Washington's pressure to increase defense spending or to stimulate internal demand. A falling German demographic curve also means that fewer recruits will be available for service in the 1990s. The perception of a receding Soviet threat further weakens incentives to increase defense expenditures.

France's implicit dependence on a strong NATO nuclear and conventional front is now threatened. A weaker NATO conventional posture reduces the time when Paris will have to decide whether to employ its nuclear weapons. In a denuclearized Europe, France's short-range tactical or pre-strategic forces, particularly its Pluton and, later, its Hadès army units with ranges, respectively, of 120 and 450 km, will have little or no room within which to maneuver (if they have not been preemptively destroyed by Soviet nuclear or conventional weapons). Room for maneuver implies access to German soil since the range of Hadès and, worse, Pluton makes West Germany rather than Warsaw Pact forces the effective target of French tactical nuclear forces. In any event, as Jacques Isnard, *Le Monde's* leading military writer, has suggested, France's pre-strategic forces will be essentially nullified as a distinct military option as they will be viewed by an adversary as essentially fused with France's strategic forces.[66]

Fifth, French economic and technological resources and the domestic consensus on which defense spending rests—calculated at less than 4 percent of GNP—[67] are now so strained that exterior assistance is needed to sustain the ambitious objectives of the latest French five-year defense plan. French means and willingness to spend more for defense fall short of current five-year plans for a follow-on system to the M-4, a new mobile missile, a full-range of pre-strategic nuclear weapons for all the armed services, a new nuclear-fueled aircraft carrier, and the replacement of the Mirage 2000, equipped with a new dual-capable air-to-ground missile—all without allied help.

French weapons planning is based on the optimistic assumption of an annual 3 percent growth rate over the next two decades. There is little likelihood that this level can be achieved, or that, if it were, France's ambitious arms modernization program could be achieved. According to the OECD, France's growth rate, one of the lowest in western Europe, averaged only 1.1 percent between 1981 and 1985. Unemployment in the late 1980s is stagnating at over 10 percent.[68] As the proportion of the defense budget devoted to nuclear weapons increases, the trend since 1981, the squeeze on France's already underequipped conventional forces will inevitably tighten. The fall in foreign orders for French arms since 1983 also increases the cost of equipment and diminishes capital available for investment in research and development.

The remaining years of the current French *loi-programme* for defense estimates a 6 percent real increase in spending for equipment, according to Prime Minister Jacques Chirac.[69] Again, these increases, if sustained, will be devoted on a priority basis to the nuclear program. Even if expenditures for conventional arms also grow, the implicit ceiling on overall defense spending as a function of an almost static GNP means that cuts will have to be found somewhere, very likely in operating expenses or in troop reductions, areas that will adversely affect France's non-nuclear posture.

France needs help on all these fronts to retain what appears to be a receding U.S. nuclear commitment and military presence in Europe, to anchor Bonn to the West, to blunt the Soviet denuclearization campaign, to sustain its position in the détente sweepstakes, and to increase allied contribution to France's arms development. A policy of the empty chair, as some influential players in the French security community recognize,[70] no longer serves French interests.

Partly in response to this changing strategic environment, successive French governments since the 1960s have, as noted earlier, slowly drawn France into closer military and political alignment with its allies (e.g., nuclear nonproliferation).[71] The new strategic environment created by recent real or perceived shifts in U.S., German, and Soviet thinking and behavior can be expected to prompt similar, if painful, revisions. Firm but sensitive U.S. leadership and tangible rewards for cooperation without a lien on independence and operational control of its nuclear forces would speed and smooth the period of adjustment.

Once France is a member of Western nuclear arms talks, with well-established credentials as a superpower critic, it can be expected to spur both superpowers to make deep cuts in their own inventories. While neither superpower now has much direct influence in shaping France's *force de frappe*, neither does France have much impact on superpower strategic policies and arms control accords that vitally affect its security. An expanded Western arms control negotiating framework could ease French fears and reassure British planners that their concerns would be addressed and that their participation in superpower arms talks would be mutually beneficial.

Possible Areas for European Cooperation

If direct U.S. overtures prove initially more a challenge than an opportunity for France to strengthen its nuclear forces and an invitation to contribute directly in reconstituting Europe's security system, then another avenue might be to facilitate direct British-French nuclear discussions. Current talks enjoy the cautious support of the Thatcher government, attentive to U.S. reactions and concerned about the special American relationship, as well as the French Ministry of Defense. Resistance to Anglo-French cooperation appears more pervasive in the French foreign office. Its encouragement would not necessarily be incompatible with expanded tripartite Western talks. With little difficulty, both states could coordinate the scheduling of their submarines on station to maximize the number of submarine patrol days. Other areas, currently ruled out, that might eventually be broached include exchange of information about target menus (as distinguished from coordinated targeting plans) and the possibility of target reporting to minimize redundancy, an acute issue for small nuclear powers. Progress on these and associated fronts will depend on Washington's support, since Great Britain is currently obliged to adhere to a complex web of restrictions about sharing U.S. technology with third parties. A favorable step in this direction, which raises fewer problems with the United States or with French concerns about loss of operating control of their nuclear forces, was the announcement by London and Paris that they are discussing development of an air-to-ground missile to arm, respectively, their Tornado and Mirage aircraft.[72]

The multiplication of Franco-British nuclear talks and cooperative ventures would also foster a long-term solution to the problems raised by European dependency on the United States. It remains a historical anomaly, as Jean-Pierre Bechter, secretary of the National Defense Committee of the French National Assembly, observed, that "320 million Europeans [whose GNP approximates that of the U.S.] can continue forever to ask 240 million Americans to defend us against 280 million Soviets."[73] While it is in the vital interest of the United States to preserve open economic and political institutions in Europe, and to be closely associated with its defense, long-term stability will be possible only when Europe's security rests on a strong European consensus.

Nudging Europe to initially adopt convergent if not congruent defense policies through closer Franco-British ties makes good strategic and political sense only if those policies are placed in a multilateral framework. Otherwise, they would have concentrated NATO's leadership in a troika composed of the Western nuclear powers potentially at the expense, and certainly without the participation, of other alliance members, most notably West Germany. Moreover, the destabilizing features of three centers of nuclear initiative and the hazards of horizontal and vertical proliferation promoted by current Western nuclear policies would not be attenuated over time. Convergence in Western nuclear policies is a precondition for positive movement toward a European deterrent, a dampening of global proliferation incentives, and the eventual reconciliation of a divided Europe.

As a start, Britain and France could pledge their deterrents to Europe's defense and specifically to Germany. London already formally assigns its nuclear forces to NATO and, more concretely, holds hostage its intentions by maintaining ground and air forces in Germany. Partly in response to French prompting, the British have also shown renewed interest in regenerating the Western European Union (WEU) as a forum for articulating European defense concerns as long as such efforts in no way weaken the U.S. military commitment to the alliance. In October 1987, both London and Paris joined their European partners, including West Germany, in adopting a common platform for European security that underscored the indispensability of nuclear deterrence.[74]

In what appears to be a critical departure from strictures first defined by President Charles de Gaulle, Gaullist Prime Minister Jacques Chirac in December 1987 publicly pledged France's military support to Bonn in a crisis. "Who can henceforward doubt, in the contingency where the Federal Republic of Germany would be a victim of an aggression, that the engagement of France would be immediate and without reserve? There cannot be one battle for Germany and one for France. It is thus in recalling its determination to fulfill its obligations that it has freely underwritten that our nation will contribute best to deterrence in Europe."[75] It is still too early to assess the extent to which this commitment constitutes an abandonment or substantial revision of France's cherished doctrines of nonautomaticity and nonbelligerency. What is clear is that it marks an important step forward in the French efforts to break out of the isolation into which its nuclear strategy has taken it. As those engaged in the French debate over nuclear weapons have increasingly recognized, France's splendid isolation was indeed isolating, leading, as some prominent French officials recognized, to its "Albanization." Other states were thus given freer rein to define Europe's (and France's) security. It would appear that French politics is slowly on the mend since the Right and the Left, however much they may have otherwise disagreed, are willing to enlarge France's participation in European and Atlantic arms control and security negotiations and even military planning, either bilaterally with Britain and West Germany or multilaterally through the WEU.

Integrating Non-Nuclear Forces into the
European Nuclear Regime

Where France has a particularly vital role to play is in linking cuts in
nuclear weapons to the non-nuclear balance in Europe, including
conventional munitions and chemical weapons. France has been
ahead on this issue since the superpowers began START and, later,
the Geneva talks on nuclear systems.[76] France is now joined by
Britain in insisting on progress in non-nuclear limitations, including
participation in arms control talks that may, with potentially
welcome effect, deemphasize nuclear weapons in Europe's defense. A
negotiated security regime for Europe that raises the nuclear
threshold and narrows the scope of nuclear weapons inevitably
focuses attention on non-nuclear forces. The arguments for and
against conventional deterrence are well known and need not be
rehearsed here. The principal utility of conventional forces is that
they buy time, forestalling nuclear escalation. Enough conventional
forces are needed by the West, moreover, to discourage a Warsaw
bloc attack under the cover of superpower nuclear stalemate.
Creation of FAR was a right step in the wrong direction since, to
finance more mobile force, French troop levels had to be reduced
by twenty-two thousand. If the costs of France's (and Britain's)
nuclear forces could be lowered through Anglo-American
collaboration, savings could be reassigned to non-nuclear forces to
minimize painful trade-offs between nuclear and conventional
preparedness.

One serious problem that needs French attention, if Paris is to
contribute to conventional arms cuts in Europe, are the roles
assigned national tactical nuclear forces. Each of France's three
services will have battlefield weapons, more as a concession to
interservice rivalry than as a coherent response to strategic needs.
These forces are too small and of too limited range to be a useful
war-fighting force (an implausible scenario for Europe where
Germany would be the battlefield), yet too large just to warn the
Soviet Union—*un coup de semonce*—that a strategic strike is in
preparation. There are four thousand tactical nuclear warheads in
NATO's arsenal as well as nuclear-capable U.S. and allied aircraft,
forces large enough, without French help or hindrance, to manage a
crisis whether deliberately or inadvertently begun, before escalation
to strategic nuclear levels is set in train.

It would be misleading, however, to suggest that the French will
easily abandon their attachment to tactical nuclear weapons,
including development of an enhanced radiation weapon or neutron

bomb. But if progress can be made on aligning French and allied arms control and military policy on other fronts, then a basis will have been created to tackle the nettling issue of the role of France's pre-strategic forces in Europe's (and France's) defense. President Mitterrand and Socialist opinion generally appear more sensitive to this issue and, specifically, to German sensibilities than either the Gaullist or Independent Republican wings of the right-of-center coalition in power between 1986 and 1988.[77]

The French can take some satisfaction in the May 1987 communiqué of the Warsaw Pact, which suggests a strong Soviet willingness to negotiate cuts in non-nuclear forces. The communiqué makes concessions in principle to French (and Western) insistence on asymmetrical cuts, given perceived Eastern bloc superiority in tanks, artillery, and interior logistical support. It also adheres to the principle of balanced forces between blocs which, if realized, would essentially preclude a surprise and shattering attack on NATO defenses. Moscow is also on record as favoring "simultaneous and parallel" cuts in non-nuclear and tactical nuclear forces. NATO denuclearization need not precede lowered conventional arms levels.[78] Open inspection, accepted in the superpower missile accord, is also reaffirmed. Even more remarkable is the shift in Soviet strategic thinking, which now concedes that security arises from reassuring potential adversaries rather than from intimidating them.

Cuts in NATO non-nuclear and nuclear forces could be more easily contemplated and absorbed if France could be counted upon from the start of a conflict, a concern somewhat eased by recent governmental pronouncements, but by no means completely allayed. Part of the price for Western support of France's nuclear modernization would be its contribution to NATO non-nuclear planning. Paris, like London, would still retain national control of its nuclear forces. Reliance on them would not be as risky or treacherous as would be the case if French forces were isolated in Europe—"Albanized"—or if NATO non-nuclear defenses were allowed to decline.

Closer bilateral Franco-German military cooperation would be especially welcome. Explicit extension of France's nuclear protection to Germany, suggested but not directly affirmed in Prime Minister Chirac's December 1987 address to high-level officials of the French security community, would facilitate closer Paris-Bonn defense collaboration.[79] It would be considered the final and logical step arising from bilateral cooperation between Paris and Bonn, evidenced by continuing military exercises, the creation of a mixed Franco-German brigade, and a military council, as well as from pledges, already made by President Mitterrand in 1986 and reaffirmed in his visit to Bonn in October 1987, that France would expect to consult with Germany about the use of pre-strategic forces to the degree that the exigencies of a crisis would permit. A closer bilateral relationship would be more appealing to many in both countries who have grounds to be skeptical of U.S. leadership. A heightened European element within the Western alliance might also blunt anti-American sentiment and strengthen the alliance by insulating it from unpopular U.S. policies or behavior outside of Europe. France in turn would be less isolated in Europe or in the alliance.

A confident West Germany, tied more closely to France and to the West, can be expected to lend its resources to what should be the third aim of Western strategy: a gradual shift in emphasis from nuclear and conventional deterrence to socioeconomic and political competition between East and West. One key objective of Prime Minister Margaret Thatcher's visit to Washington in July 1987 was to encourage the U.S. leadership to seize on the opportunity for a fundamental relaxation of the East-West conflict. The possibility of such a bargaining synergism, linking military, nuclear and non-nuclear, economic, and technological concessions by both sides, within a context of improved political relations and increased economic and cultural exchange, has never been so present since the start of the Cold War. Prime Minister Thatcher, who had extensive and far-ranging talks with Soviet Party Secretary Mikhail Gorbachev during her March 1987 visit to Moscow, is apparently convinced that "great changes are taking place in the world, including historic changes in the Soviet Union. It is a time of unprecedented opportunity," said the British Prime Minister in her brief visit to the United States in July 1987, "if we are wise and skillful enough to grasp it."[80] If the United States widens its negotiating stance toward the Soviet Union by incorporating the interests and counsel of its principal allies in Europe, a new era in Soviet-American relations can conceivably be opened.

Exploiting Soviet Weakness for Mutual Benefit

There is growing evidence that the pervasive need for technoeconomic and sociopolitical reform within the Soviet Union creates powerful incentives for a relaxation of the conflict with the West and for a slowing of the arms race. NATO countries with a GNP greater than twice the Warsaw Pact (three times if Japan is included) and with a military establishment that checkmates the East can bargain from a position of strength in negotiating lowered nuclear and non-nuclear force levels and an easing of East-West tensions, as well as in multiplying the number and enlarging the scope of exchanges of people, goods and services, and ideas across the ideological divide. A rare opportunity exists for the West to exploit Soviet internal weaknesses for mutual advantage. Attention and priorities can be progressively directed away from lethal toward nonlethal forms of competition. Time and resources can be reallocated from external concerns to make long-overdue repair of tattered domestic fabrics and to improve the quality of life in the East and West.

To get the Soviet nation and economy moving again appears to require several major shifts in Soviet foreign and security policy. With an economy approximately half that of the United States, it spends about 15 percent of its GNP for unproductive military purposes. This high level of expenditure slows the civilian economy and, worse, reduces the resources available for investment and future technoscientific and industrial development.

The January 1986 party paper to eliminate nuclear weapons, however much an effective propaganda and diplomatic instrument to advance Moscow's denuclearization campaign, can also be read as a domestic reform document.[81] Cutting spending first for nuclear arms makes sense given the superpower stalemate. An arms accord that slows the nuclear arms race, especially in defensive systems where Moscow believes that the United States has an advantage, would relax the economic and technological burdens of the East-West conflict without essentially undermining U.S.-Soviet parity.

Adoption of the double-zero option, while not necessarily weakening Western defenses, would still not essentially change the threat to the Western alliance of Soviet long-range nuclear and non-nuclear forces. These threats can only be diminished by deep cuts in both categories of weaponry. The Soviet Union can be induced to contemplate such cuts, at a pace and in a form of the West's choosing, if the latter uses its technological and economic advantages as leverage. Trade-offs between the East and West, while never easy, are not enhanced by keeping nuclear, non-nuclear, and technoeconomic negotiations and bargaining insulated from one another. A strengthened Western defense and arms control position, as outlined above, is the precondition for a broad-based diplomatic offensive once Western nuclear and non-nuclear deterrence regimes are more coherently defined and enjoy more widespread governmental and popular support on both sides of the Atlantic than they do today. The Western states will be in a position to elicit Soviet concessions on non-nuclear forces as well as on a broad range of issues currently separating East and West. As a bonus, the Soviet economy would be engaged within a Western-dominated system. A lost opportunity of the Marshall Plan, to keep the East open to a Western-dominated global economy and susceptible to its Western influence, might now be reclaimed forty years later.

Why should the Soviet Union go along and why should the West be forthcoming? Besides cuts in military spending, the Soviet Union needs access to Western products and know-how. Widening trade, increasing Western credits and investment, and multiplying technological transfers imply a relaxation of the East-West arms race and political tensions. A top-heavy Soviet economy, based on an administratively determined price system, is demonstrably incapable of setting priorities or investing efficiently. Since internal centralization and bureaucratization limit the degree to which competition can be domestically generated to reduce distortions, the cold bath of external competition is needed to make Soviet industries and managers more efficient. Changes recently instituted by the Gorbachev regime to permit greater flexibility and freedom from bureaucratic control of its commercial agencies and an expansion of joint ventures with capitalist firms abroad signal the need for foreign help and for the stimulus of competition to enhance the managerial efficiency and the quality of products issuing from Soviet industry.

A competition based on conflicting Soviet and Western expectations on who will be the final winner of increased socioeconomic and political competition should hardly be frightening. Such competition plays to the West's strong suit. Drawing the Soviet Union into an increasingly interdependent world, already proclaimed in official party pronouncements as a new strategic reality,[82] poses serious dilemmas for the maintenance of the Soviet state in its present form and for control of its European empire. Opting for an opening to the West is an open admission of the fading attraction of the Soviet model for other countries. Moscow places itself in competition with its clients for Western favor. It is by no means certain that its present strategy of moving westward while attempting to consolidate its hold over Comecon states will be successful. Decentralization of economic planning and resource allocation, moreover, will inevitably weaken internal party and bureaucratic control as new centers of power and authority are created. In accommodating itself to a nonsocialist world economy, the Soviet Union risks diluting its revolutionary fervor and commitments and losing its socialist soul. The West did not create these contradictions. Its interest is in drawing profit from them through peaceful but competitive engagement framed by a negotiated security arrangement acceptable to the superpowers and to their European allies.

Conclusions

The last step along the arduous path toward integrating British and French forces into the superpowers balance must be clear before the first step makes sense to the European nuclear powers. Current superpower negotiations are too narrowly conceived to be attractive to London or Paris. Conversely, if the reservations of the West European nuclear powers are incorporated into the strategic thinking and arms control negotiations of the superpowers, progress can be made in slowing the arms race (deep cuts, constraints on defensive systems, lower British-French nuclear levels); in multiplying the number and expanding the scope of confidence-building measures (e.g., notification of military exercises or the expansion of on-site inspection); in dampening the incentives for armed conflict and rapid escalation should hostilities erupt (improved Western and East-West signaling); in narrowing gaps and in eliminating costly redundancies in Western nuclear and non-nuclear strategy and operational readiness (a more reliable and multilaterally constructed Western deterrent with increased emphasis on conventional deterrence and preparedness); in strengthening governmental, elite, and popular support for Western defense policy (greater national responsibility for alliance policies within a less threatening regional security system); in decreasing European dependence on the United States (gradual emergence of a European deterrent); and in contributing to the gradual transformation of Western Europe's security regime. In the latter instance, Soviet intentions can be tested by linking greater economic and technological exchange to decreases in Soviet non-nuclear capabilities. If the Soviet Union through internal reform gradually accommodates itself to a multipolar system, the European security that is currently directed *against* the Soviet Union can progressively be redefined to one built on socioeconomic and political competition *with* the cooperation of the Soviet Union.

A serious problem confronting U.S. (and Soviet) arms diplomacy and statecraft—powerful independent nuclear systems in Europe— can be turned to opportunity and advantage. Addressing British concerns about neglected up-links between European nuclear forces and those of the superpowers, prompted by an unregulated superpower arms race and given specific point by SDI, would relax the contradictions between U.S. nuclear policies and behavior and the independence, invulnerability, and penetrability of these forces. Incorporating French (and German) insistence on down-links between superpower nuclear and bloc non-nuclear forces would also increase U.S. sensitivity to continental European worries about exposure to Soviet pressures if the denuclearization of the European theater does not move synchronously with cuts in nuclear and non-nuclear capabilities and the expansion of confidence measures like those reached on East-West oversight of military exercises within the framework of the Conference on Security and Cooperation in Europe (CSCE). The CSCE forum, incidentally, is favored by Paris and Moscow for non-nuclear talks over the Mutual and Balanced Force Reduction negotiations in Geneva; U.S. adhesion to the CSCE as a negotiating framework to discuss conventional arms cuts could reduce inner-allied friction. Greater peaceful engagement between East and West might also feed back to lower pressures to expand the military requirement of European security on both sides.

A superpower arms control process, supplemented by an expansion of Western nuclear and non-nuclear arms control negotiations, would reintroduce Europe into the process of European security and détente. The United States must apparently relearn how to negotiate with its allies over matters of vital interest to them. Consultation in the form of unilateral pronouncements and faits accomplis have obviously not generated alliance confidence nor fostered coherent responses to Soviet initiatives. Rifts in alliance thinking and planning are now routinely inspired either by superpower conflicts—whether in Europe (e.g., INF deployments) or outside (U.S. bombing of Libya or Kuwaiti reflagging)—or by superpower accord (e.g., double-zero option). In much the same way that arms control between adversaries should be considered a long-term process of adjustment to changing internal political and external strategic needs and weapons modernization imperatives, alliance nuclear policymaking should also be conceived as an ongoing process in which the members have varying leverage to help or hinder an ally's aims. However much the Western allies may be collectively committed to mantaining open societies, they have, at the margin, differing socioeconomic and strategic interests, conflicting views about how to respond to external challenges, and dissimilar and often cross-cutting internal support structures, themselves the product of the vicissitudes of history and conjunctural democratic politics. A winning Western strategy assumes a delicate balance between effective military, socio-economic, and diplomatic responses to external imperatives, continuing cohesion among allied governments, and sustained domestic support for all of the above. Allied cooperation cannot be commanded. It can only be elicited as a function of satisfying exchanges of benefits among allies in much the same way that superpower arms control accords must rest on mutual interests.

Progress will not be easy, quick, or cheap; much less will it be the result of altruistic appeals to alliance solidarity. No one accord among the Western states or between the East and West will ensure stability or peace. The centrifugal forces moving the European states and superpowers apart are too compelling to be contained or constrained by any one agreement or statement of common purpose. Independent European nuclear forces and the national wills that inform and direct them—among some of the most powerful operating today in the international arena—can be harnessed to the service of European regional and global security and cooperation only if the serious concerns of millions of Europeans that underlie them are used to moderate the superpower conflict, the latest and potentially the most dangerous of a series of failed attempts over the past several centuries by one or more nation-states for global domination.

Notes

1. Descriptions of the Trident program can be found in several sources, including Lawrence Freedman, *Britain and Nuclear Weapons* (London: Macmillan, 1980); Peter Malone, *The British Nuclear Deterrent* (London: Croom Helm, 1984); E. R. Hooton, "The United Kingdom TRIDENT Programme," *Military Technology*, January 1986, pp. 14–28; and Stockholm International Peace Research Institute (SIPRI), *World Armaments and Disarmament: SIPRI Yearbook 1987* (London: Oxford University Press, 1987), pp. 22–26.

2. Robert S. Norris, "Counterforce at Sea: The Trident II Missile," *Arms Control Today* 15, No. 7 (September 1985), pp. 5–10.

3. Speech of Rt. Hon. George Younger, Secretary of State for Defense, to the Royal Institute of International Affairs, 11 March 1987, p. 18. See also Roy Dean, former director of the Arms Control and Disarmament Research Unit, Foreign and Commonwealth Office in *The World Today*, September 1983, pp. 319–322. The eight-warhead limit derives from the decision to load the British D-5 with no more warheads than the C-4 Missile (Trident I) which had been initially contracted for by the Thatcher government. Partly to blunt domestic critics that Britain was heading toward a counterforce, first-strike system, the Thatcher government confined D-5 to C-4 limits.

4. William Hill, "384 Warheads for UK Trident Force," *Jane's Defence*

Weekly, 9 June 1984, pp. 913–917. Not all analysts assume these conservative estimates. See Paul Rogers, *A Guide to Britain's Nuclear Weapons* (London: CND Publications, 1985), pp. 16–17.

5. French strategic forces and corresponding sources are described in greater detail with notes and sources in Edward A. Kolodziej, *Making and Marketing Arms: The French Experience and Its Implications for the International System* (Princeton: Princeton University Press, 1987), pp. 107–132.

6. "France's ASMP Nuclear Cruise Missile Operational," *Military Technology*, July 1986, pp. 62–71.

7. Eric J. Grove, *Where and When? The Integration of British and French Nuclear Forces with the Arms Control Process*, Faraday Discussion Paper No. 5 (London: Council for Arms Control, 1985), p. 21.

8. U.S. Department of State, *Bulletin* 48, No. 1229 (14 January 1963), p. 44.

9. Letter of Prime Minister Margaret Thatcher to President Ronald Reagan, quoted in John Baylis, *Anglo-American Defence Relations, 1939–1984*, 2d ed.. (London: Macmillan, 1984), p. 202.

10. U.S. Department of State, *Bulletin* 48, No. 1229 (14 January 1963), p. 44.

11. Quoted in William Kaufmann, *The McNamara Strategy* (New York: Harper and Row, 1964), p. 117.

12. Arthur Schlesinger, Jr., *A Thousand Days* (Boston: Houghton-Mifflin, 1965), pp. 842–866, and Richard Neustadt, *Alliance Politics* (New York: Columbia University Press, 1970).

13. See memoirs of Harold Wilson, *Labour Government, 1964–70: A Personal Record* (London: Weidenfeld & Nicolson, 1971), passim.

14. U.S. Department of State, *Bulletin* 71, No. 1828 (8 July 1974), pp. 37-44.

15. Speech of Rt. Hon. George Younger, 11 March 1987, p. 14.

16. See Manchester *Guardian*, 7 June 1987.

17. See letter of President Ronald Reagan to Prime Minister Margaret Thatcher, quoted in Baylis, p. 203.

18. Ibid.

19. United Kingdom, Secretary of State for Defence, *Statement on the Defence Estimates 1986*, Command Paper 9763-II (London: HMSO, 1986), pp. 11–13.

20. See, for example, Wilfrid Kohl, *French Nuclear Diplomacy* (New York: Columbia University Press, 1971); Michael M. Harrison, *The Reluctant Ally: France and Atlantic Security* (Baltimore: Johns Hopkins University Press, 1981).

21. See, for example, France, Ministère de la Défense, *La Politique de défense de la France*, Dossier d'Information No. 75 (October 1984), p. 22.

22. See note 20 and David S. Yost's thoroughgoing *France's Deterrent Posture and Security in Europe*, Part 1: *Capabilities and Doctrine*, Adelphi Paper No. 194. (London: International Institute for Strategic Affairs [IISS], 1985). Also helpful for the current debate is Robbin Laird, ed., *French Security Policy: From Independence to Interdependence* (Boulder, Colo.: Westview Press, 1986).

23. These concerns are reflected, for example, in the speech of Raymond Barre, a former prime minister and candidate for the French presidency, in the annual Alastair Buchan lecture of the International Institute for Strategic Studies, 26 March 1987. For a transcript, see *Survival*, July-August 1987, pp. 271–300.

24. Kolodziej, *Making and Marketing Arms*, pp. 148–167.

25. Robert Hutchinson, "Chevaline: UK's Response to Soviet ABM System," *Jane's Defence Weekly* 2, No. 23 (15 December 1984), pp. 1068–1069. See also note 1.

26. Great Britain, Ministry of Defence, *Britain's Strategic Nuclear Force: The Choice of a System to Succeed Polaris*, Document 80/23 (London, 1980), p. 6.

27. Ibid., pp. 5–6.

28. For an analysis of alternative French and British targeting scenarios, see John Prados, et al., "The Strategic Nuclear Forces of Britain and France," *Scientific American* 255, No. 2 (August 1986), pp. 33–41. British and French targeting strategies are also extensively covered, respectively, in Lawrence Freedman, "British Nuclear Targeting," in Desmond Ball and Jeffrey Richelson, eds., *Strategic Nuclear Targeting* (Ithaca, N.Y.: Cornell University Press, 1986), pp. 109–126; and in the same book David S. Yost, "French Nuclear Targeting," pp. 127–156.

29. Ibid.

30. A recent MIT simulation of a Soviet attack on the United State finds that hitting the energy-producing and maintenance infrastructures would delay recovery by decades. See M. Anjali Sasty, et al., *Nuclear Crash: The U.S. Economy after Small Nuclear Wars* (Cambridge: Program in Science and Technology for International Security, MIT, 1987). Conversely, a U.S. attack on Soviet energy resources would presumably also have a devastating effect on the Soviet Union and a retarding effect on recovery.

31. General Jeannou Lacaze, "La politique militaire," *Défense Nationale*, November 1981, p. 15.

32. *Times* (London), 3 March 1987. For a confirming view, see Ivan Tyolin and Andrei Zagorsky, "Dimensions of a 'Near-Zero' Nuclear Balance," *International Affairs* (Moscow) 7 (1988), 111–114, 142ff.

33. Quoted in the statement by Roy Dean, *The World Today*, September 1983, p. 321. Italics added.

34. France, Assemblée Nationale, *Projet de loi de programme relatif à l'équipement militaire pour les années 1987–1991*, No. 432 6 November 1986, p. 11. The Chirac Government adopted the same view as the preceding Socialist administration.

35. See the remarks of Foreign Minister Jacques Cheysson, quoted in David S. Yost, *France's Deterrent Posture and Security in Europe*, Part 2: *Strategic Arms Control Implications*, Adelphi Paper No. 195 (London: International Institute of Strategic Studies, 1985), p. 53.

36. Quoted by Malone, *The British Nuclear Deterrent*, p. 118.

37. France, Assemblée Nationale, Commission de la Défense Nationale et des Forces Armées, *Projet de loi portant approbation de la programmation militaire pour les années 1984–1985*, No. 1485 (May 1983), p. 91. See also Charles Hernu, "Equilibre, dissuasion, volonté: la voie étroite de la paix et de la liberté," *Défense Nationale*, December 1983, p. 15.

38. Quoted in France, Sénat, Commission des Affaires Etrangères, *Rapport d'information sur l'initiative de défense stratégique*, No. 449, (10 July 1986), p. 96.

39. *Projet de loi de programme, 1987–1991*, No. 432, p. 11.

40. Interviews, London, January-April 1987 and speech of Rt. Hon. Geoffrey Howe, secretary of state for Foreign and Commonwealth Affairs, to the International Institute for Strategic Studies, 27 January 1987, pp. 8–10. See also the joint U.S.-British communiqué of 15 November 1986, issued on the

occasion of Prime Minister Thatcher's visit to the United States, known as Camp David II: "We confirmed that NATO's strategy of forward defence and flexible response would continue to require effective nuclear deterrence, based on a mix of systems. At the same time, reductions in nuclear weapons would increase the importance of *eliminating conventional disparities.* Nuclear weapons cannot be considered in isolation, given the need for stable overall balance at all times." Press Release of the British Embassy (Washington, D.C., 15 November 1986). (Emphasis added.)

41. See the views of Jean Villars, a pseudonym of a high official in the Ministry of Foreign Affairs, "Un parapluie en dentelle ou la dissuasion nucléaire et l'alliance atlantique après l'option zéro," *Politique Internationale,* No. 37 (Fall 1987), pp. 124–135. Former Minister of Defense André Giraud was also widely quoted as critical of the treaty (*Le Figaro,* 17 October 1987).

42. See the speech of Prime Minister Jacques Chirac before the Institut des Hautes Etudes de Défense Nationale, 12 December 1987, pp. 5–7. "It is significant," said the prime minister, "...that the [INF] treaty precedes an accord on the reduction of strategic arsenals which would have logically constituted, for the superpowers, the first task of disarmament as I have had occasion to recall in Washington and in Moscow."

43. Address of Sir Geoffrey Howe, secretary of state for Foreign and Commonwealth Affairs, before the UN General Assembly, 28 September 1983, p. 6.

44. See press release of the British Embassy (Washington, D.C.), 15 November 1986.

45. Speech of Rt. Hon. Geoffrey Howe, secretary of state for Foreign and Commonwealth Affairs, 14 March 1985.

46. Ibid.

47. Speech of Rt. Hon. Geoffrey Howe, secretary of state for Foreign and Commonwealth Affairs, 27 January 1987, p. 20.

48. Speech of Prime Minister Margaret Thatcher, Moscow, 30 March 1987, p. 7.

49. For a review of French reaction to SDI, see John Fenske, "France and the Strategic Defense Initiative: Speeding Up or Putting on the Brakes?," *International Affairs* (London) 62, No. 2 (Spring 1986), pp. 231–246. The clever logic and conflicting interests underlying French behavior are discussed at length in the report of the French Senate cited in note 38.

50 See the report of the American Physical Society, *Science and Technology of Directed Energy Weapons,* April 1987.

51. Catherine McCardle Kelleher, "NATO Nuclear Operations," in Ashton B. Carter, et al., eds., *Managing Nuclear Operations* (Washington, D.C.: Brookings Institution, 1987), pp. 445–469.

52. François Heisbourg, "Défense française: l'impossible statu quo," *Politique Internationale,* No. 36 (Summer 1987), pp. 137–153.

53. Dan Caldwell, "Permissive Action Links," *Survival* 29, No. 3 (May-June 1987), pp. 224–238.

54. SIPRI, *World Armaments and Disarmament: SIPRI Yearbook 1987,* pp. 22–26.

55. See note 42, pp. 1–2.

56. See the author's "Nuclear Weapons in Search of a Role: Evolution of Recent American Strategic Nuclear and Arms Control Policy," in Paul R. Viotti, ed., *Conflict and Arms Control* (Boulder, Colo.: Westview Press, 1985), pp. 3–23.

57. See, for example, the evaluation of U.S. strategic policy and arms control initiatives presented to the French National Assembly: France, Assemblée Nationale, Commission de la Défense Nationale et des Forces Armées, *Avis sur le projet de loi de finances pour 1988. Défense, espace et forces nucléaires*, No. 963, 8 October 1987, pp. 22–23.

58. Quoted in Villars, "Un parapluie en dentelle," p. 130.

59. See note 42. Doubts about the efficacy of Western strategy or about long-term governmental and public support have also arisen in Britain and France.

60. Even in Thatcher's Britain, criticism of U.S. defense policy is mounting. See Simon Duke, *US Defence Bases in the United Kingdom* (London: Macmillan, 1987). While William K. Domke, Richard Eichenberg, and Catherine Kelleher find less cause for alarm about the domestic political supports for NATO than other analysts, they also concede deep rifts in the popular opinion of member states on NATO's nuclear policy. William Domke, et al., "Consensus Lost: Domestic Politics and the 'Crisis' in NATO," *World Politics* 39 No. 3 (April 1987), pp. 382–407. For a French view, see François Heisbourg, "Europe/Etats-Unis: le couplage stratégique menacé," *Politique Etrangère*, No. 1 (Spring 1987), pp. 111–127.

61. See Kohl and Harrison, note 20, and Edward A. Kolodziej, *French International Policy under De Gaulle and Pompidou: The Politics of Grandeur* (Ithaca, N.Y.: Cornell University Press, 1974).

62. David Gress, *Peace and Survival* (Stanford, Calif.: Hoover Institution Press, 1985). See also François-Georges Dreyfus, "RFA: le péril national-neutraliste," *Politique Internationale*, No. 37 (Fall 1987), pp. 185–200, and in the same issue Renate Fritsch-Bournazel, "L'Ostpolitik et l'effet Gorbatchev," pp. 205–215.

63. Pierre Hassner, "L'Europe sans options?" *Politique Internationale*, No. 37 (Fall 1987), pp. 97–110.

64. See Mikhail Gorbachev, "Statement by the General Secretary of the CPSU Central Committee," in *For a Nuclear Free World* (Moscow: Novosti Press, 1987), pp. 7–22.

65. See Dreyfus, "RFA: le péril national-neutraliste."

66. *Le Monde*, 24-25 October 1987, p. 2.

67. For an analysis, see Kolodziej, *Making and Marketing Arms*, pp. 143–147.

68. Organization for Economic Cooperation and Development, *France* (Paris, 1987), appendix.

69. See note 42.

70. See Heisbourg, "Défense française" and Pierre Lellouche, *L'avenir de la guerre* (Paris: Mazarine, 1985), passim, for a critique of France's empty-chair policy and of the need for greater allied support given economic and political constraints on defense spending.

71. See Bertrand Goldschmidt, "Le contrôle de l'énergie atomique et la non-prolifération," *Politique Etrangère* 42, Nos. 3-4 (1977), pp. 413–430.

72. *Le Monde* 16 December 1987. See also Heisbourg, "Défense française," pp. 146–147.

73. Quoted in the *Washington Post*, 13 July, 1987, p. A13.

74. Interviews, London, January-April 1987; see also *Western European Union Platform on European Security Interests*, The Hague, 27 October 1987 [and Le Prestre, this book. Ed.]. Note should be taken of serious Italian reservations about WEU. Italy in no way wishes to give the United State an

excuse to weaken its forces or commitments in Europe nor to find itself in a subordinate position within a revitalized WEU.

75. Note 42, p. 12. Emphasis is that of prime Minister Chirac.

76. Yost, *France's Deterrent Posture*, Part 2, p. 44ff.

77. See statements of President François Mitterrand during his visit to Germany 18–21 October 1987. Contrast these with former Prime Minister Jacques Chirac, note 42, who underscored the military significance of those arms, a view then shared by his Minister of Defense André Giraud.

78. *Actualité Soviétique* (Paris), No. 121, 5 June 1987. *Communiqué de la Conférence du Comité Politique Consultatif de l'Organisation du Traité de Varsovie*, p. 4.

79. Heisbourg, "Défense française," p. 150, and Lellouche, *L'avenir de la guerre*, p. 279ff. For an analysis that tends toward the same conclusion although it stops short of advising the extension of the French nuclear guaranty to West Germany, see the penetrating paper by Thierry de Montbrial, director of the Institut Français des Relations Internationales, "Sur la politique de securité de la France," August 1987, mss. [See also Brigot in this book for a discussion of German and French attitudes regarding this possibility. Ed.]

80. British Embassy of the United States, *Test of the Statement Made by the Prime Minister*, The Rt. Hon. Margaret Thatcher at The White House, 17 July 1987, p. 1.

81. See note 64.

82. See the selection "From the Political Report of the CPSU Central Committee to the 27th Party Congress," in Gorbachev, pp. 37–46. The foreign policy implications of the "new political thinking" in the Soviet Union and its roots in Soviet reform efforts are discussed with insight by Charles Glickman in "New Directions for Soviet Foreign Policy," *Radio Liberty Research Bulletin*, 6 September 1986. Also valuable in exposing the connection between Soviet economic policy and foreign policy behavior is Elizabeth Valkenier, The Soviet Union and the Third World: An Economic Bind (New York: Praeger, 1983).

Index _____